PERGAMON INSTITUTE OF ENGLISH (OXFORD)

English Language Teaching Documents

General Editor: C. J. BRUMFIT

DICTIONARIES, LEXICOGRAPHY AND LANGUAGE LEARNING

British Council ELT Documents published by Pergamon Press

Back Issues (published by the British Council but available now from Pergamon Press):

Special Issues and Occasional Papers

DICTIONARIES, LEXICOGRAPHY AND LANGUAGE LEARNING

Edited by

ROBERT ILSON
University College London

ELT Documents 120

Published in association with
THE BRITISH COUNCIL
by
PERGAMON PRESS
Oxford · New York · Toronto · Sydney · Frankfurt

U.K.	Pergamon Press Ltd., Headington Hill Hall, Oxford OX3 0BW, England
U.S.A.	Pergamon Press Inc., Maxwell House, Fairview Park, Elmsford, New York 10523, U.S.A.
CANADA	Pergamon Press Canada Ltd., Suite 104, 150 Consumers Road, Willowdale, Ontario M2J 1P9, Canada
AUSTRALIA	Pergamon Press (Aust.) Pty. Ltd., P.O. Box 544, Potts Point, N.S.W. 2011, Australia
FEDERAL REPUBLIC OF GERMANY	Pergamon Press GmbH, Hammerweg 6, D-6242 Kronberg-Taunus, Federal Republic of Germany

First edition 1985

Library of Congress Cataloging in Publication Data

Main entry under title:
Dictionaries, lexicography, and language learning.
(ELT documents; 120)
1. Lexicography.   2. Language and languages—Study and teaching.
I. Ilson, Robert.   II. British Council.   III. Series: English language teaching documents; 120.
P327.D54 1985   413'.028   84-25430

British Library Cataloguing in Publication Data

Dictionaries, lexicography and language learning.
—(ELT documents; 120)
1. English language—Study and teaching—Foreign speakers   2. English language dictionaries
I. Ilson, Robert   II. British Council   III. Series
420'.7   PEII28.A2
ISBN 0-08-031084-2

Printed in Great Britain by A. Wheaton & Co. Ltd., Exeter

PREFACE

There seems no reason to challenge the first statement in this book, Robert Ilson's contention that "The dictionary is the most successful and significant book about language." Very few people these days avoid dictionaries completely, and almost everyone who has tried to learn a language in formal circumstances will have used one on many occasions. Yet we know little about the uses to which dictionaries have been put by learners and teachers, and much teacher education passes over the use of the dictionary in embarrassed silence.

This may be partly because it is easier to recognize the dangers of misusing dictionaries than the dangers of ignoring them. But all of us in language teaching need to understand more about them, for they are the most widespread single language improvement device ever invented. We cannot prevent our students using them, but we can ensure that they are used wisely.

Robert Ilson's collection is probably the most complete survey of pedagogically relevant lexicographical issues ever published. Any teacher or learner can examine this to find out the basic principles of language, design, and educational use of dictionaries. Lexicographers will find much information about various forms of dictionary, as well as discussion of the implications for learners of particular forms of organization. All members of the language professions will benefit from greater understanding of our key institutions, and the dictionary is probably the most taken for granted of all these.

C. J. BRUMFIT

CONTENTS

PART III. APPLICATIONS OF AND ALTERNATIVES TO DICTIONARIES

PART IV. FROM THEORY TO PRACTICE

INTRODUCTION

ROBERT ILSON

University College London

The dictionary is the most successful and significant book about language. In Britain, its success is shown by the fact that over 90% of households possess at least one, making the dictionary far more popular than cookery books (about 70%) and indeed significantly more widespread than the Bible (which was to be found in 80% of households in England in 1983, according to the Bible Society). Its significance is shown by the fact that—like the Bible—its authority is invoked, rightly or wrongly, to settle disputes, and by the fact that, quite spontaneously, I wrote "the dictionary" and "the Bible" (rather than "dictionaries" and "Bibles") but "cookery books" (rather than "the cookery book"). For us English-speakers, the contents of the dictionary are part of the normative social discourse that helps to constitute, maintain and give identity to our speech community. In this very fundamental sense, another analogy with the Bible is possible: in reference to the dictionary, too, we may be called "peoples of the Book".

The dictionary discussed so far, however (though it almost certainly accounts for most of the 90%), is only one type of dictionary. It is the monolingual general dictionary for the adult native speaker of English. Each of the phrases used to describe it suggests what other types of dictionary there are. There are bilingual dictionaries as well as monolingual ones. There are specialized dictionaries—covering a part of the language, such as idioms or the technical terminology of one or more areas—as well as general ones. There are dictionaries for children as well as dictionaries for adults. There are dictionaries for learners as well as dictionaries for native speakers. And the learners need not be learners of English. Now one begins to speak of "dictionaries" rather than of "the dictionary"

A book about dictionaries could take any of these types as its starting-point. *This* book is part of a series called *ELT Documents*, and, accordingly, its point of departure is the monolingual general dictionary for the adult learner of English. In some respects this starting-point is fortunate, for we now know in general terms what an ideal learners' dictionary should do. It should model the lexical competence of the adult native speaker. However abstract and incomplete our knowledge of that competence is, however difficult it is to embody that knowledge in real learners' dictionaries, it is doubtful whether we have an equivalent idea of what any other type of dictionary should do.

Among the authors of the essays collected in this volume are lexicographers, linguists and language-teachers from several countries, including people associated with some of the principal dictionary publishers in Britain.

I

We begin by comparing EFL learners' dictionaries with dictionaries of other types: with native-speaker dictionaries (see Kirkpatrick), bilingual dictionaries (see Atkins) and learners' dictionaries of French (see Lamy). These essays raise a number of practical questions, of importance to people working with all three genres.

How different are learners' dictionaries and native-speakers' dictionaries? Samuel Johnson intended his dictionary of 1755 to be useful to both groups. To that end he devoted special care to the treatment of what we now call phrasal verbs, and was at pains to include in his explanations synonyms of both Romance and Germanic origin for their values as cognates, "that every learner of *English* may be assisted by his own tongue". Today, many French dictionaries are explicitly addressed to both natives and learners, as Lamy points out. And it is a fact that many English native-speaker dictionaries are bought by people for whom English is a second language, which is one reason why more and more British native-speaker dictionaries are using the International Phonetic Alphabet (IPA) to show pronunciation.

How different are learners' dictionaries and bilingual dictionaries? Can learners' dictionaries incorporate translation glosses as well as definitions (as some of them already do)? This would be in line with the increasing practice of producing language-specific or region-specific EFL courses rather than global ones intended for everybody. Conversely, if people in fact use bilingual dictionaries as learners' dictionaries, and not "just" as translation aids, to what extent should bilingual dictionaries do things that learners' dictionaries do—such as pay greater attention to the syntactic behaviour of the words they translate?

How international is lexicography, indeed? English-speaking and French-speaking lexicographers have much to learn from one another. Furthermore, there are now monolingual learners' dictionaries not only for English and French, but also for Russian, German, Spanish and Dutch, at least. Though many features of dictionaries are language-specific, many are not, and it is to be hoped that such developments as the formation in September 1983 of EURALEX, the European Association for Lexicography, reflect an awareness that lexicographers in many different countries have many similar problems.

Limitations of space prevented the inclusion in this volume of material about two of the other principal types of dictionary: the terminological dictionary and the children's dictionary. That is a pity, because both deserve examination in a book of this kind.

The terminological dictionary is relevant for two reasons above all. The first reason is its frank confrontation of one of the central problems of lexicography: the relation between the lexicographic treatment of words and their encyclopaedic treatment; that is, broadly speaking, the difference between their intra-linguistic sense and their extra-linguistic reference. The second reason is the way terminological dictionaries deal with the sets formed by terms, both those relating to entities of the natural world (such as chemical elements) and those naming man-made concepts (such as government departments or university ranks): culture-bound concepts notoriously hard to translate.

As for the children's dictionary, its relevance to the learners' dictionary should be apparent. A comparison of the lexical needs of the native learner (the child) and the foreign learner is very much in keeping with the general comparison now going on of first-language acquisition and second-language learning. But there are more down-to-earth reasons for considering the children's dictionary here. It has been, especially in American lexicography, what the EFL dictionary has been in British lexicography: a centre of innovation. American children's dictionaries have pioneered in the use of unorthodox defining techniques, the creative use of examples to complement and sometimes to replace definitions, the imaginative use of pictures, and, perhaps most interesting of all, under the inspiration of E. L. Thorndike, the grouping together of semantically related senses across part-of-speech boundaries, as when the military senses of *charge* are explained next to each other even though some are nominal and some are verbal (see in this connexion the remarks on *arrest* in Atkins's essay). Furthermore, children's dictionaries have developed a number of devices for helping their users to acquire "the dictionary habit", and their writers have also created guides for teachers using the dictionaries with their pupils. But at this point a major problem must be faced: the children's dictionaries under discussion are intended for *younger* children, and there are as many differences between dictionaries for younger and older children as there are between different types of dictionary for adults.

II

The second section of this book concerns parts of dictionaries. The essays here are presented more or less in the order in which their subjects would affect the lay-out of an actual dictionary (though there is, alas, no separate essay on etymology). So word-formation, which, as it were, creates headwords, comes before pronunciation, which is shown for headwords thus created (see Stein on word-formation, Wells on pronunciation).

Much of the information in this section is relevant to dictionaries of all types. Even the terminological dictionary, for example, may benefit from the results of investigating collocations, for the tendency to use the terms *fortis* and *lenis* of consonants but *tense* and *lax* of vowels is not unlike the collocational or selectional association of *addled* with *eggs* and *rancid* with *butter* or *bacon*.

It is in this section that the importance of communication between lexicographer and linguist is particularly striking. Thus, if linguists can teach lexicographers about the syntactic behaviour of words (see Jackson), lexicographers can teach linguists about the behaviour in word-formation of so-called combining forms, which for some time now have been treated in many dictionaries differently from prefixes and suffixes but are only now gradually attracting the attention from linguists they deserve (see Stein). Similarly, though linguists have long proclaimed the value in principle of studying collocations, it was the need to describe actual words in specimens of an "Explanatory and Combinatorial Dictionary" that enabled Mel'čuk and his colleagues to develop an explicit framework for investigating them (see Benson). And though lexicographers have long been aware of the value of gathering citations as evidence about actual usage (including collocations), the computer can now provide far more of this sort of evidence than previous generations of lexicographers could hope to obtain (see Sinclair).

The essays by Sinclair and Bolinger in this section make fascinating reading as a pair. They illustrate the delicate interplay between subjectivity and objectivity, between intuition and evidence, that is the essence of sound lexicography. Both Bolinger and Sinclair give appreciative but critical attention to the judgements of past dictionaries. But Bolinger illustrates the value of what Geoffrey Broughton has called "native-speaker insight" in teasing out the various uses of -*less* while Sinclair shows, in his treatment of *decline*, how insight can be enriched by the evidence that computers can provide, leaving us with a portion of that evidence in the form of two Appendices that we can interpret and explore in the spirit of Richard Wilbur's Copernicus, who tested his hypotheses, "Not hesitant to risk/His dream-stuff in the fitting-rooms of fact. . . ."

Whitcut's essay connects the first and second sections of this collection by discussing a *feature* of dictionaries, the Usage note, which is found in dictionaries of more than one *type*. She also points the way to the third section of the collection when she asks "the thousand-dollar question": "But How Will They Know Where To Look It Up?" Dictionaries have in the past too often been considered simply as systems of information storage. Too little attention has been devoted to the problem of information retrieval. Do people know what is in dictionaries? Can they find it? And, if they find it, can they use it?

We know far too little about the cognitive strategies of dictionary use. I, for example, will look up senses I believe to be new near the end of a polysemous entry rather than near the beginning. If most people follow the same strategy, the implications for sense-ordering are significant. But at the moment we simply do not know what most people do.

III

The third section of this book deals with applications of and alternatives to dictionaries. Working with dictionaries is very much a question of information retrieval, in its two senses mentioned above: (1) Can the information be found? (2) Can the information be used? People who write workbooks to accompany dictionaries must be aware of the important distinction adumbrated by Lamy, between activities that acquaint people with the structure of their dictionaries and activities that help people to use for their own purposes the information their dictionaries contain. At the same time, the essays by Rossner and Underhill suggest that some activities can compass both ends; especially, perhaps, those activities that encourage people, as it were, to think about language lexicographically. Advanced learners might well be encouraged to play with Sinclair's appendices and come to their own conclusions about how *declined* is used. They might, indeed, be encouraged to compare the way the texts they are studying use words and the way those words are treated in their dictionaries, and even to accumulate their own "citation files".

If Underhill and Rossner make us think about information retrieval, Hill raises important questions about information storage as well. Basically, dictionaries store information alphabetically; thesauruses and pictorial dictionaries store information conceptually. But there is more than one way to do this. Information may, for example, be stored by real-world situation (as in Hallig and Wartburg's *Begriffsystem als Grundlage der Lexikographie*—or Tom McArthur's *Lexicon*) or by more abstract "notions" (as in Roget's conceptual schema). Perhaps it can be stored by "functions" as well. New developments in information science may suggest other possibilities and improvements of existing schemes. But whatever the underlying principle adopted by a non-alphabetic language book, it is likely to be supplemented by an alphabetic index for ease of information retrieval. Nevertheless, the converse also happens: alphabetic dictionaries use many devices for transcending their special sort of linearity; for example, cross-references (most systematically in the French *Robert* dictionaries) and composite illustrations and tables. And in their compilation, dictionaries may be written, at least in part, in sets of related items rather than in strictly alphabetical order. In this book, too, a system of cross-references has been introduced, so that readers can see what different authors have to say about related subjects.

IV

Dictionaries are social artefacts, existing in the real world and compiled in "real time". Their shape is determined not just by linguistic theory or lexicographic style, but by administrative necessity. McGregor's essay is an attempt to acquaint lexicographers and the wider public with how dictionary projects are actually managed. People who want better dictionaries (and better thesauruses, too, for that matter) must begin to consider how their proposals can be put into practice. If, for example, it is desired to write sets of related items together, how can that method of compilation be *scheduled*?

Closely related to such questions, though not discussed in this book for reasons of space, is the problem of the selection, training and professional development of lexicographers. The dictionary is a recognized institution, but lexicography has yet to become a recognized profession. The formation of EURALEX is a major step in this direction, as was the formation in 1975 of its transatlantic counterpart, DSNA, the Dictionary Society of North America. Perhaps this very book, whose starting-point is the EFL dictionary, will encourage people to consider whether the professionalization of EFL, so welcome an advance of the past 20 years, might appropriately be paralleled by the professionalization of lexicography.

I. TYPES OF DICTIONARY

A LEXICOGRAPHICAL DILEMMA: MONOLINGUAL DICTIONARIES FOR THE NATIVE SPEAKER AND FOR THE LEARNER

BETTY KIRKPATRICK

Chambers Publishers

Few things, if any, can be all things to all men—or to all women for that matter. This is as true of books as it is of anything else and it is particularly true of dictionaries. It is impossible for any one dictionary to satisfy the needs of everyone, wide-ranging and diverse as these needs are.

Yet there is a popular belief, prevalent among at least the lay members of the public, that one dictionary is much like another and that as long as they have such an object safely tucked up somewhere in their bookshelves they have provided all the linguistic help their family is ever likely to require. The idea that dictionaries might vary in any way from each other is as alien to these people as the idea that dictionaries ever change.

For this reason do they refer not to dictionaries but to "the dictionary" in much the same way as they refer to "the Bible". Both of these essential works of reference are considered to be ultimate in their authority, but the Bible has fared slightly better in terms of linguistic folklore. Most people are at least vaguely aware that some versions of the Bible have changed slightly in terms of language. Not so the hapless dictionary. It is thought never to alter even "when it alteration finds".

Theoretically such views of dictionaries—or rather of "the dictionary"—should have changed radically by now. Heaven knows, enough dictionaries have been published recently with all the concomitant publicity brouhaha. How could the general public fail to notice the lavish advertisements in the press, the jargonistic "point-of-sale material" carefully placed at the tills of their local bookshops, the spectacular window-displays, the expensive if ephemeral television advertising? Easily enough it seems. Indeed just as easily as they have stumbled over great piles of new dictionaries in bookshops without noticing them.

Of course not all the recent dictionary drum-banging has been in vain. Certainly more people than before are aware that not all dictionaries are the same, although I suspect that even some of these harbour cynical and sceptical doubts. They probably see the whole thing as publishing hype and who can blame them since so much has been made of the odious phrase "dictionary war" to describe the competition between dictionary publishers? A dictionary should be a force for peace, a dove not a hawk, should it not?

Those of us who work in the field, toiling as we spin, so to speak, are in no doubt about the differences between one dictionary and another. Dictionaries are definitely not the same as one another. Just as there are genres of novel, so are there genres of dictionaries. It is more than time that people were made aware of that.

This distinction between genres of dictionary is nowhere more evident than that which exists between dictionaries which are intended primarily for use by those whose mother tongue is English—or a dialect of English—and dictionaries which are designed for those who are learning English as a foreign or second language. Of course the story does not end there.

The genres are further subdivided almost *ad infinitum* according to the level of ability and sophistication of the user. The use to which he or she intends to put the dictionary must also be taken into consideration. Earnest lexicographers, for example, especially those working on dictionaries for native speakers of a language, must remember that not everyone uses a dictionary for serious purposes. If they should forget this, all that slaving over hot dictionaries will be in vain.

Many native speakers purchase dictionaries for leisure purposes. They use them to help them solve crossword puzzles or to help them to confound their opponents in other word-puzzles, such as Scrabble. Dictionaries help them in their word battles.

Not to be forgotten either are the users who simply enjoy wandering down the byways and the path-ways of their native tongue. One word will lead them to another, one etymology engender their interest in another and so on. Many people regard a dictionary as good bedside material and not just because it helps stabilize the wobbly leg of their bedside table.

A sense of humour is probably more vital in people working on dictionaries for native speakers than in those working on dictionaries for foreign learners. Johnson, father of lexicography, set a trend for idiosyncratic, humorous definitions which the British public at least seem to approve of. Certain it is that when some definitions of this genre which had been in previous editions of *Chambers Twentieth Century Dictionary* were removed in 1972 the public were so incensed that they wrote to the national press.

Apart from this humorous aspect of dictionaries, what are the major differences between the perfect dictionary for speakers of English as a mother-tongue and the perfect dictionary for learners of English as a foreign language? Even laying aside the fact that no-one, least of all rival publishers, is ever going to agree on what constitutes perfection there is much scope for argument and disagreement on this topic. Most people would admit that the

International Phonetic Alphabet

differences referred to do in fact exist, but the nature of the differences might cause controversy.

Take pronunciation for example. It is generally acknowledged that most learners of English as a foreign language are used to learning how to pronounce words through the medium of IPA. For a while, of course, that brought its own particular problems when what was popularly known as DJ 14 appeared—the Gimson edition of Daniel Jones's famous *Everyman's English Pronouncing Dictionary*. [Cf. Wells, this volume, p. 50, list 3—Ed.]

phonetics

Some British publishers of dictionaries for learners of English as a foreign language adopted it immediately. Publishers of dictionaries in other countries, notably Sweden, shared the same enthusiasm. Others were slower to follow suit.

The reason for this was probably simply that so many teachers were used to the previous system—known as DJ 13. Having learnt this as man and boy—or woman and girl—they were reluctant to learn a whole new system of symbols. In the midst of all this there was a further not unimportant factor to be taken into consideration.

Many of the English textbooks, at least in European countries, used the long-favoured DJ 13. Education boards are notoriously reluctant to spend money on new things when the old things are going along seemingly satisfactorily. Perhaps we cannot blame them, although one can take conservatism too far.

Meanwhile back at the native-speaking dictionary ranch most people were sticking to the various forms of pronunciation schemes known as respelling schemes, schemes that avoid for the most part the symbols of the IPA system—except for the occasional schwa—and instead make use of the ordinary letters of the Roman alphabet.

Admittedly it was not long before the odd publisher—odd not in the sense of strange I hasten to add—decided that the time was ripe to expose the great British public to the delights of the symbolic IPA system, but it cannot, with any great degree of truth, be said to have made much impact. Indeed it could be said that IPA was a non-event for the native speaker. So much so indeed that one of the latest new dictionaries for the mother-tongue market hails their respelling scheme in such a way as to suggest that this is a novel idea.

The question of pronunciation in dictionaries for native speakers does not appear to be nearly so important as it is in dictionaries for learners of English. I have been working on native-speaking dictionaries for many years and it is my impression that very few people regularly use general English dictionaries to establish pronunciation except for the occasional controversial word—like *controversy*.

When the native speaker does turn to a dictionary for help with pronunciation he/she appears to have either an antipathy towards, or a lack of understanding of, phonetic symbols. If they have not studied a foreign language at school they will be totally unfamiliar with such symbols and many would prefer to go in ignorance of how to pronounce the word rather than consult the prefatory material for the detailed explanation of the symbols. Idleness is a difficult disease to cure!

Some publishers have an understandable cynicism about what I am claiming to be the great British public's attitude to pronunciation schemes. Presumably they feel that anyone can get used to anything in time. However, I have good evidence to put forward in support of my claim. Over the years several people, one very recently, have written to point out that all the "e's" in our pronunciations are upside down. They refer of course to the schwa—that indispensable indicator of unaccented vowels—and one of the few non-members of the Roman alphabet in our respelling scheme.

So much for pronunciation. What other potential differences must one bear in mind when approaching the two different types of dictionary? One of the most important of these is definitions. They are, after all, central to dictionaries. I have already touched earlier in this article on the subject of idiosyncratic definitions.

Space—or lack of this commodity—is always an acute problem in dictionaries, whatever the type or size. It affects both vocabulary coverage and number and length of definitions. A curious fact of life, however, is the fact that buyers of dictionaries and reviewers, whether academics or not, seem to think that every single dictionary should contain absolutely everything, including a vogue phrase coined the day before publication, irrespective of the size, aims or claims of the dictionary.

I should point out in passing that when I refer to dictionaries for native speakers in this article I am thinking primarily of high-vocabulary dictionaries for the reasonably sophisticated user. When I refer to dictionaries for learners of English as a foreign language I am exempting those users who are so advanced in English as to be virtually native speakers.

Taking up the thread of definitions once more, I feel that, for the most part, learners' dictionaries require definitions which are couched in simpler language than dictionaries for native speakers do. The problem is that it takes more space to define something in simple terms than it does to define something in more difficult and succinct terms. This inevitably cuts down on the number of words that can be dealt with.

This seems as good a point as any to introduce a topic that does not really concern dictionaries for native speakers but is an issue of some controversy with regard to dictionaries for learners of English as a foreign language. I refer to the system of defining known as the limited or restricted vocabulary system.

In other words, the definer will use only the words contained in a specified list to define any word that is in the dictionary. The idea, of course, is that the user will familiarize himself or herself with all the words in the specified list and so will automatically understand all the definitions. Relatively minor problems will, of course, arise such as should the definer assume that the user will be able to cope with all the derivatives of the words in the defining word list. For example, if *medicine* is in the list will the user understand the word *medically*?

Like so many other things the defining vocabulary scheme is fine in theory, not so in practice. The worst feature of the defining vocabulary system is the constraints that it places on the definer. A restricted vocabulary system definitely runs the risk of producing definitions phrased in language which sounds most unnatural and so of encouraging the reader to emulate this. You know how convincing the printed word is! The other problem is that it is virtually impossible to define some words, especially technical words, in terms of a limited vocabulary list.

Another problem relating to space and so to vocabulary coverage is worth considering. The various senses and subsenses require to be much more clearly differentiated in a learners' dictionary than in its native speakers' equivalent. Developed and extended meanings and figurative usages are much more understandable to native speakers than they are to foreign learners, provided of course that the native speakers are acquainted with the core meaning of the word concerned.

Then, of course, there are words that have to be treated in much greater detail in learners' dictionaries than in native speakers' dictionaries—the much-dreaded function or structure words. Thankfully these need only be dealt with scantily in native speakers' dictionaries. It is for this reason that lexicographers who write for the home market look for the most part younger than those who have battled through the minefields of *in*, *of*, *for*, etc.!!

Perhaps everyone should conclude that these are basically undefinable. It would save a lot of headaches. In any case one frequently finds the absurdity that one has to use the word that one is meant to be defining in the definition of that word.

At this point someone is bound to point out that it is not the definitions of function words that are important but the examples of usage. As long as the foreign learner receives enough help from the illustrative sentences or phrases it will not matter so very much if he or she is unable to cope with the maze of definitions. Arguably, showing how these words are actually used is what counts.

Most one-volume dictionaries for native speakers of the type previously described in this article do not deal in any depth with examples of usage, although some add a few, often in a fairly haphazard way. This absence of wholesale examples of usage in dictionaries for native speakers seems perfectly reasonable.

For one thing, copious examples would detract inevitably from the large volume of vocabulary demanded by users of such dictionaries. For another a great deal of language—whether or not everyone would deem it correct language—comes instinctively to one whose mother tongue it is, in a way that it does not to the foreign learner. The same form of guidance is not necessary.

Occasionally, users of dictionaries for native speakers put in a plea for short examples to illustrate words with which they have particular difficulty— whether to say *different from* or *different to*, when should *continuous* really be *continual*, what is the difference between *infer* and *imply*, and can *aggravate* be used interchangeably with *irritate*? Interestingly enough many of the words such readers ask about are either cases where the distinction between the relevant words has gone or they are grey areas where the distinction is on its way out—to howls of protest.

Examples of usage, although undeniably useful to the learner of English, tend to be a source of concern to me and I would imagine that this concern would be shared not only by people who have worked on dictionaries for foreign learners but by any native speaker who has ever even glanced through the pages of one such volume. Cries of "but I would never say that" or "but that is just not English" are almost bound to issue from the lips of this last category.

It is difficult to think up examples of usage especially when under the stress of a deadline and when one has just survived the trauma of actually defining the word. Using written citations is not necessarily the answer because writers and journalists like to play around with the language in a way that would sound not quite right from a non-native speaker. Using the unusual is the mark of a skilled and confident writer.

Unnatural-sounding examples of usage are not a phenomenon of any particular dictionary—just a hazard of the genre. Of course there are several safety nets to prevent such examples slipping through. The problem is that these safety nets are editors or advisers and it is very difficult to get native English speakers to agree on what is natural-sounding English. Arguments have been known to ensue for hours.

I do not wish to cause undue stress to foreign learners. For the most part examples of usage are thoroughly reliable. It is just that they are like cars—you get the odd Friday-afternoon one, but not many. Have every confidence in learners' dictionaries!

Just as examples of usage are more necessary in dictionaries for foreign learners than in those for native speakers so are register and field labels. Such labels are invaluable to learners as they indicate to them the context and situations in which particular words or meanings are appropriate or inappropriate. This can save a great deal of embarrassment and confusion.

The extent and nature of the labelling system varies from one learners' dictionary to another but most will label in some way or other words which are formal or literary, words which are informal or slang and words which are offensive or taboo. This last category is particularly important. Of much less importance are labels like sport, chemistry or medicine since the appropriate context is usually deducible from the definition.

The question of register labels is much less important in dictionaries for native speakers and is generally not dealt with in any depth. Native speakers, simply from their own experience of using and speaking the language, are less likely to make mistakes of the formal/informal kind. Interestingly enough many dictionaries for native speakers still label slang words although the distinction between slang and non-slang becomes ever more elusive.

Dictionaries for native speakers frequently indicate whether a word or a meaning is archaic or obsolete. This is not so common in dictionaries for foreign learners as the vocabulary coverage does not often include many such words, the average learners' dictionary being an aid to the use of English rather than to the reading of English.

These then are some of the major differences between dictionaries for native speakers and dictionaries for foreign learners. I cannot, however, end this article without expressing my amazement at how quickly learners of English as a foreign language "grow out" of the dictionaries designed for them and become such accomplished users of the language that they require the greater vocabulary coverage of the dictionary for the native speaker. People whose mother tongue is English hardly ever reach these heights in a foreign language. Shame on us!

MONOLINGUAL AND BILINGUAL LEARNERS' DICTIONARIES: A COMPARISON

BERYL T. ATKINS

Collins Publishers Ltd

These dictionaries, both designed for use by non-native speakers of at least one language, differ in one fundamental way: monolinguals, being non-user-language specific, must cater for users of any native language, while no such demand is made upon bilinguals. From this stem many radical differences in design, content, presentation, accessibility to the student, and potential as an aid to L2 production.

However, one further point must be made: within the general context of an L2 dictionary, one work, whether bi- or monolingual, may differ in its specific aim from another of the same type. It may be simply a *dictionary of comprehension* (allowing the student to understand L2) or it may be a much more ambitious *dictionary of communication* (comprehension and production of L2). Major bilingual dictionaries nowadays tend to be what J. Rey-Debove terms *réciproque* (JRD), that is to say they are designed as dictionaries of communication for a native speaker of either language. This, however, is not normally the case when one language has world-wide currency and the other is geographically restricted, for example English and Swedish. Such a dictionary is usually intended principally for the minority user. This may be readily appreciated from the following entries for "*bitch*" and "*hynda*" (NKL):

bitch [*bitʃ*] hynda, sköka; förstöra, fuska bort   **hynda** bitch

The Swedish user will have no difficulty in appreciating the full extent of *bitch*, whether in the literal or figurative sense of the noun, or the colloquial verb. Pity the poor English user who, wishing to express *bitch* in Swedish, must consult the entries for *hynda* ("bitch"), *sköka* ("harlot"), *förstöra* ("spoil") and *fuska bort* ("botch up"), and who will find no help with the pronunciation, inflections or syntactic patterning of any of these Swedish words.

Space considerations prevent any further consideration of the dictionary of comprehension alone; the rest of this article will be devoted to an examination of the dictionary of communication, undoubtedly a more satisfactory teaching aid. To ensure a consistent framework, illustrations will be taken only from dictionaries in which the L2 is English, and comparisons made only between works of approximately the same coverage.

A dictionary entry will consist of some or all of the following components in something like the following order, which may be compared with Janet Whitcut's (JW's) presentation in this volume:

15

(1) the headword, and any variant spellings (cf. JW's 2);
(2) an indication of pronunciation (cf. JW's 3);
(3) details of the word classes (parts of speech) to which the headword belongs (cf. JW's 4);
(4) morphology: inflection(s) which may cause difficulties (cf. JW's 5);
(5) syntax: the syntactic potential of the headword and any syntactic restrictions it may carry;
(6) an explanation of the various senses of the headword;
(7) exemplification of usage, including collocating words and fixed or semi-fixed phrases (e.g. idioms) (cf. JW's 10 and 11);
(8) a listing of derived forms of the headword, with or without further explanation (cf. JW's 13);
(9) cross-reference(s) to related entries.

In addition, there may be metalinguistic information of several types:

(10) semantic (including selectional restrictions): allowing the user to identify the specific sense being treated at any particular point, or otherwise clarifying the design and content of the entry (cf. JW's 8 and 9);
(11) stylistic: indication of style and register, where relevant (cf. JW's 7);
(12) usage material for the purpose of further clarification, e.g. differentiation from near-synonyms, or warning of hidden hazards;
(13) etymological: a diachronic view of the headword (cf. JW's 12).

Of these components, Nos. 2, 3, 4 and 9 show no systematic variation between mono- and bilingual dictionaries, and No. 13 rarely occurs in current (synchronic) works for the learner. The way in which the others are realized, however, in these two types of dictionary reflects fundamental differences in concept and design, and conditions the effective use which a student may make of the book.

(1) and (8) Headword and Derivatives

Bilingual and monolingual learners' dictionaries do show systematic variations in their approach to the wordlist (the stock of vocabulary items to be treated). In a monolingual, no attempt is made to cover the whole vocabulary, the assumption being that having mastered the most frequent words in the language the learner will graduate to a native speakers' dictionary. Bilinguals have generally a much more flexible approach to the wordlist, which may vary from the few thousand most frequent items (in a beginners' dictionary) to coverage as full as that of any native speakers' monolingual. Also, of course, bilinguals contain not one but two discrete wordlists (L1 and L2).

Criteria for headword (as opposed to derivative) status vary with every individual dictionary, and one cannot generalize about this, as may be seen from the various ways in which *lend* and its derivatives *lender, lending, lending library, lend-lease, lend out* and the more debatable *lendable* are treated in the following dictionaries, all evidently written for learners in much the same state of advancement:

(a) Monolingual (ALD)

lend /lend/ *vt* (*pt,pp* lent/lent/) **1** [VP6A, 12A, 13A, 14] ~ **sth to sb,** ~ **sb sth,** give (sb) the use of (sth) for a period of time on the understanding that it or its equivalent will be returned: *I will ~ you £100, but I can't ~ money to everyone.* ~ **a hand (with sth),** help. ' ~ **ing-library,** one from which books may be borrowed. **2** [VP14] ~ **sth to sth,** contribute: *facts that ~ probability to a theory.* **3** [VP14] ~ **oneself to sth,** give; accommodate: *Don't ~ yourself to such dishonest schemes. This peaceful garden ~s itself to* (=is favourable for) *mediation.* ~ **er** *n* person who ~s.

(c) Bilingual (NECD)

lend [lend] (lent [lent]) ● *vt.* ① 把…借给: They *lent* us their pumps. 他们把水泵借给我们。② 贷(款); 出租(书籍等) ③ 提供; 给予; 给: ~ support to 向…提供支持 / Social imperialism invented the theory of "limited sovereignty" to ~ legality *to* its aggression. 社会帝国主义炮制"有限主权论"为其侵略制造合法化的借口。/ The presence of the new students ~s a vigorous revolutionary atmosphere *to* the campus. 新学员的到来给校园带来了朝气蓬勃的革命气氛。/ ~ sb. a box on the ear 打某人一记耳光 ● *vi.* 贷款 ‖~ *itself* *to* 有助于, 适宜于: The rural environment *lent itself to* the restoration of his health. 农村环境有助于他恢复健康。/ ~ *oneself* *to* 帮助; 屈从: ~ *oneself to* dishonest schemes 参与诡诈勾当 ‖~**able** *a.* 可供借(贷)的 / ~**er** *n.* 出借者;贷方

lending ['lendiŋ] *n.* ①出借; 出租 ②借出物; 租借物 ‖~ **library** ①收费图书馆 ②[英](图书馆的)借书处; 公共图书馆

lend-lease ['lend'li:s] **I** *n.* 平等租借交换: the *Lend-Lease* Act (一九四一年美国制定的)租借法 **II** *a.* ①由租借法批准的 ②批准租借法的 **III** *vt.* 根据租借法供给

(b) Monolingual (LDOCE)

lend /lend/ *v* lent /lent/ **1** [D1 (*to*); (T1)] to give (someone) the possession or use of (something, such as money or a car) for a limited time: *Can you lend me £10?* **2** [D1 (*to*); (T1)] to supply (someone) with (something) on condition that it or something like it will be returned later: *As the shops are shut I'll lend you some bread* **3** [D1 (*to*); T1] to give out (money) for profit, esp. as a business **4** [T1 (*to*); (D1)] to add or give: *The many flags lent colour to the streets* **5 lend oneself/one's name to** to let oneself agree to be part of (an unworthy action) **6 lend itself/themselves to** (of things) to be suitable for **7 lend a hand (with)** to give help (with) **8 lend an ear** *old use* to listen—compare BORROW; see LOAN[2] (USAGE)—~**er** *n*

lending li·bra·ry /'··,··/ *n* a library which lends books, music, etc.

(d) Bilingual (CGD)

lend [lend] *pret, ptp* lent **1** *vt* **(a)** (*loan*) leihen (*to sb* jdm); (*banks*) *money* verleihen (*to an +acc*). **(b)** (*fig: give*) verleihen (*to dat*); *name* geben. **I am not going to ~ my name to this** dafür gebe ich meinen (guten) Namen nicht her; **to ~ a hand** helfen, mit anfassen. **2** *vr* **to ~ oneself to sth** sich für etw hergeben; (*be suitable*) sich für etw eignen. ♦ **lend out** *vt sep* verleihen; *books also* ausleihen.

lender ['lendə^r] *n* (*professional*) Geldverleiher *m*. **he returned the £100 to the ~** er gab die £ 100 an den zurück, der sie ihm geliehen hatte.

lending ['lendiŋ] *adj library* Leih-. ~ **rights** Verleihrecht *nt*; (*for author*) Anspruch *m* auf Leihbücherei-Tantiemen.

lend-lease ['lend'li:s] *n:* ~ **agreement** Leih-Pacht-Abkommen *nt*.

These extracts raise one point of interest for anyone choosing an L2 dictionary: are the criteria for headword status accessible to the non-native speaker? How is the user for whom English is L2 to divine that the derived form *verb-headword+-er* or *-r* is to be treated as a sub-entry at *lend* but as a full headword in the case of *compute* (this is true of (a), (b) and (c) above)?

(3) Grammatical Classification and its status within the entry

The flavour of a dictionary is set at the moment when the grammar is given priority over the semantics (or vice versa) as a basis for classification. In both the following cases, the headword *arrest* has been analysed first on grammatical and subsequently on semantic grounds:

(a) Monolingual (CULD)

arrest [ə'rest] *vt* **1** to capture or take hold of (a person) because he or she has broken the law: *The police arrested the thief.* **2** (*formal*) to catch or attract (a person's attention): *My attention was arrested by a sudden movement.* **3** (*formal*) to stop: *Economic difficulties arrested the growth of industry.—nc* **1** the act of arresting or being arrested (*eg* by the police): *The police made several arrests during the football match.* **2** (*tech*) a stopping of action: *Cardiac arrest is another term for heart failure.—See also* **under arrest** *below.*

(b) Bilingual (GEJD)

*ar·rest [ərést] 圖 ⑥ ＜とらえる＞ ❶ を逮捕する，検挙する． ～ the criminal 犯人を逮捕する． ～ a man *for* drunken driving 飲酒運転で男を逮捕する． He was ～*ed on* suspicion of murder. 彼は殺人容疑で逮捕された． ❷ ＜とらえて動きをとめる＞〔進行を〕止める，遅らせる，(check)． Still pictures ～ the motion of a moving object. スチール写真は動く物の一瞬の動きをとらえる． ～ economic growth 経済成長にブレーキをかける． ❸ ＜とらえて放さない＞〔注意，人の目を〕引く． ～ a person's attention 人の注意を引く． —— 圖 ⓤⓒ ❶ 逮捕，検挙. a warrant for his ～ 彼の逮捕令状. make many ～*s* 多くの人を逮捕する. ❷ 《医·法》停止，中断；阻止. a cardiac ～ 心拍停止. *under arrést* 逮捕されて[た]. place [put] a person *under* ～ 人を逮捕する. You're *under* ～. おまえを逮捕する《警察官の言葉》.

This is the standard approach in most dictionaries. These priorities could however be reversed, as the following crude scissors-and-paste adaptation of the CULD entry shows:

> **arrest** [ə'rest] *vt* **1** to capture or take hold of (a person) because he or she has broken the law: *The police arrested the thief.* —*nc* **1** the act of arresting or being arrested (*eg* by the police): *The police made several arrests during the football match.* **2** (*formal*) to catch or attract (a person's attention): *My attention was arrested by a sudden movement.* **3** (*formal*) to stop: *Economic difficulties arrested the growth of industry.* **2** (*tech*) a stopping of action: *Cardiac arrest is another term for heart failure.—See also* **under arrest** *below.*

The obvious objection to this has already been raised, namely that the basis on which decisions are made, viz. the sense of the *definiendum*, is by definition (saving the expression) rarely available to the user. Against this, it must be said that a primary "cut" through the word on the basis of sense rather than grammar leads to a much more economical entry. One could for example reduce the adapted CULD entry to:

1 vt to capture or take hold of (a person) because he or she has broken the law: *The police arrested the thief.* **1.1** nc *The police made several arrests during the football match.* **2 vt** to catch or attract (a person's attention): *My attention was arrested by a sudden movement.* **3 vt** (*formal*) to stop: *Economic difficulties arrested the growth of industry.* **3.1** nc (*tech*): *Cardiac arrest is another term for heart failure.*

This is also a considerably more elegant description of *arrest*, allowing the user to make the same connections across word-class boundaries as those made instinctively by the native speaker on the Clapham omnibus.

It is worth noting that here, as in other areas, children's dictionaries have been more innovative than dictionaries for adults. In the words of Allen Walker Read (AWR): "It is usual to treat the different parts of speech as separate lexical entries, as in 'to walk' and 'to take a walk', requiring a parallel list of senses, but Edward Lee Thorndike, in his school dictionaries, experimented with grouping the parts of speech together when they had a similar sense." Here, for example, is the entry for *arrest* in the (American) Thorndike-Barnhart *Scott, Foresman Beginning Dictionary* (SFBD):

> **ar rest** (ə rest′), **1** seize by authority of the law; take to jail or court: *The police arrested the burglar.* **2** a stopping; seizing: *We saw the arrest of the burglar.* **3** stop; check: *Filling a tooth arrests decay.* **4** catch and hold: *Our attention was arrested by a strange sound.* 1,3,4 *verb*, 2 *noun*.

(6) Division into semantic categories (senses), with explanations

Another fundamental point of difference between mono- and bilingual dictionaries: in the former the explanation takes the form of a definition (in L2), while in the latter that of an equivalent, or series of equivalents, in the target language. In this instance, one extract from a bilingual no longer suffices. In order to assess the scope of a "reciprocal" dictionary, parallel entries from both sides of the book must be studied:

(a) Bilingual E–F (CRCFD)

drug [drʌg] **1** *n* drogue *f*, stupéfiant *m*; (*Med, Pharm*) médicament *m*; (*fig*) drogue. **he's on ~s** (*gen*) il se drogue; (*Med*) il est sous médication; (*fig*) **a ~ on the market** une marchandise invendable. **2** *cpd:* **~ addict** drogué(e) *m(f)*, toxicomane *mf*; **~ addiction** toxicomanie *f*; **peddler** *or* **pusher** revendeur *m*, -euse *f* de drogue; **~ runner** trafiquant(e) *m(f)* de drogue; **~ running** *or* **traffic** trafic *m* de la drogue *or* des stupéfiants. **3** *vt person* droguer (*also Med*); *food, wine etc* mêler un narcotique à. **to be in a ~ged sleep** dormir sous l'effet d'un narcotique; **~ged with sleep** abruti de sommeil.

(b) Bilingual F–E (CRCFD)

drogue [drɔg] *nf* drug. **la ~** drugs. ♦ **drogué, e** *nm, f* drug addict. ♦ **droguer** (1) *vt malade* (*péj*) to dose up; *victime* to drug. **Il se drogue** he's on drugs, he's taking drugs.

(c) Monolingual (CELD)

drug [drʌg] *nc* **1.** any substance used in medicine. **2.** substance which has a harmful effect on the mind or body. Also *vt* add or give a drug to (usu. to make somebody fall asleep). *He drugged my drink. He drugged me. past* **drugged.**

No wonder students notoriously prefer the bilingual to the monolingual dictionary! But of course teachers notoriously fear that bilinguals simply reinforce the translation barrier and thus prevent the internalization of L2—though few would go so far as the Scottish schoolteacher I met who told first-year beginners to "go and look it up in the Micro Robert" because "even if they don't understand a word of it they are at least reading French". Such a belief in language acquisition by finger contact with the printed word must be rare indeed.

(7) Exemplification of usage

(a) Monolingual (LDOCE)

poke[2] *v* **1** [X9;L9] to push sharply out of or through an opening: *His elbow was poking through his torn shirt* SLEEVE. |*She poked her head round the corner* **2**[T1 (*with*); I∅] to push (a pointed thing) into (someone or something): *You nearly poked me in the eye with your pencil.*|*Stop poking (me)!* **3** [T1] to move (the wood or coal) in (a fire) about with a POKER[1] or other such object **4** [X9, esp. *in, through*] to make (a hole) by pushing, forcing, etc.: *His large key had poked a hole in his pocket* **5** [X9; (T1)] *infml* to hit with the hand closed **6 poke fun at** to make jokes against **7 poke one's nose into something** *infml* to enquire into something that does not properly concern one.

(b) Bilingual (HSFED)

poke[3] **I.** *v.tr.* **1.** (*a*) pousser (qn. qch.) du bras, du coude; piquer (qch.) du bout (d'un bâton); **to p. s.o. in the ribs,** donner une bourrade (amicale) à qn; (*b*) **to p. a hole in sth.,** faire un trou dans qch.; crever qch. (avec le doigt, etc.). **2.** tisonner, attiser (le feu). **3.** mettre, fourrer (qch.) (**into,** dans); **to p. one's head through the window,** passer la tête par la fenêtre; *F:* **to p. one's nose into other people's business,** fourrer son nez dans les affaires d'autrui. **4. to p. fun at s.o., sth.,** se moquer de qn, qch.

It is difficult to believe that French users will grasp as much from the monolingual, with its L2 definitions and glosses, and even unglossed non-transparent usages (*She poked her head round the corner*) as they will from the L1 equivalents of the bilingual—though full marks to LDOCE for doing what many monolingual and few bilingual dictionaries attempt: distinguishing between straightforward examples of usage (*His elbow was poking through his torn shirt sleeve*) and idiomatic expressions (*poke fun at, poke one's nose into something*).

(10), (11) and (12) Metalanguage

For the user of a monolingual dictionary, all the vital metalinguistic information is in a foreign language. In the case of bilinguals, the material needed by User A is exactly what is *not* needed by User B, and vice versa; a good bilingual will aim this material at the user who needs it, and select the metalanguage accordingly.

(a) Bilingual I–E (CSID)

villa *f.* **1** (*casa di campagna*) (country-)house, villa. **2** (*casa unifamiliare di lusso*) (town-)house. □ *andare in* ∼ to go to (one's place in) the country.

(b) Bilingual E–F (CRFD)

villa ['vilə] *n* (*in town*) pavillon *m* (*de banlieue*); (*in country*) maison *f* de campagne; (*by sea*) villa *f*.

(c) Monolingual (CULD)

villa ['vilə] *nc* a type of detached or semi-detached (*usu* luxury) house, *usu* in the country or suburbs, or used for holidays at the seaside: *They have a villa in the South of France.*

In the case of (a) it is the Italian, not the English, users who need to be sure of picking the correct English equivalent for the particular type of *villa* they have in mind (*country-house* or *town-house*). The bracketed notes in Italian ensure this.

In the case of the English headword *villa* in (b), it is the English users who must distinguish between the various types (town or country), but the French users who require the information "de banlieue" to pinpoint the "villa" *pavillon* rather than the *pavillon* which is a "gatekeeper's lodge", or the one which is a "hospital ward".

In the case of (c) however, it is the non-native English speakers who have to understand, if they are to use the English word correctly, the rather difficult definition "a type of detached or semi-detached (*usu* luxury) house, *usu* in the country or suburbs, or used for holidays at the seaside". Such a definition may possibly fulfil the aims of a dictionary of comprehension; it will hardly increase the student's capacity to produce L2. (This not an attack on my friend Betty Kirkpatrick and her team—the word has an 18-line entry in the longer LDOCE (including a 7-line usage note), and ALD and CELD, both suffering from space restrictions, fare no better than CULD.)

*   *   *   *   *

Such a brief scuttle through the salient points of divergence between these two types of learners' dictionaries inevitably does justice to neither—but, equally, I hope, favours neither at the expense of the other. I have tried to pick out the aspects of an entry where these two dictionaries offer a choice to the user:

—wordlist (usually shortish in monolinguals; often longer in bilinguals);
—explanation of senses (L2 definition in monolinguals; L1/L2 equivalents in bilinguals);
—exemplification of usage (sometimes glossed in L2 in monolinguals; usually translated in bilinguals);
—treatment of fixed and semi-fixed phrases (always glossed or defined in L2 in monolinguals; always translated, often by equally idiomatic equivalent expressions, in bilinguals;
—semantic and usage information (always in a foreign language in monolinguals; usually in the user's native language in bilinguals).

What conclusions may be drawn about these two types of dictionary? Both help in understanding a foreign language, but there can be little doubt that a bilingual makes fewer demands upon the user. With a monolingual, the student is forced to *use* the foreign language in order to *understand* it, and there is of course no guarantee that the definitions, examples (glossed or unglossed) or metalanguage notes are comprehensible. In the case of a bilingual, however, target language equivalents are given for headwords, derived forms and examples, and the metalanguage is L1; the student thus uses L1 in order to understand L2.

When it comes to translation from L1 into L2, a good bilingual will supply enough information to allow students to do this reasonably correctly, while a bad bilingual will at least help them along part of the way. A monolingual learners' dictionary is in my view of little use for this operation.

Again, when students are trying to express themselves in L2, for example writing an essay or a letter, the monolingual offers little immediate help, and demands much more from its users than does a bilingual, where students may take L1 as the *point de départ*. Users of a monolingual L2 dictionary can access the material in it only by means of a foreign language headword. It might be just that word that they do not know. If that is the reason for the difficulty, the situation becomes circular, and there is no way out.

Consequently, there can be little surprise at the reluctance of most students to reach for the monolingual if there is a bilingual at hand. Yet, while students perversely prefer bilinguals, their teachers are for the most part struggling to wean them from these predigested manuals on to the more adult fare of the monolinguals. Monolinguals are good for you (like wholemeal bread and green vegetables); bilinguals (like alcohol, sugar and fatty foods) are not, though you may like them better.

Perhaps the simile is more apt than it seems. Students like bilinguals because they bring instant satisfaction, while teachers prefer monolinguals for their long-term benefits: the user gradually learns to operate in L2 without the L1 barrier as a brake on progress.

One further point on this subject: there is in the English-speaking world a fairly rigid dichotomy between monolingual and bilingual learners' dictionaries. Such is not the case in other areas: in Italy, for example, the hybrid dictionary (one with both bi- and mono- features) is a normal event. Here, perhaps, is the direction we ourselves should be moving in. If we were to combine the best features of the monolingual and the bilingual dictionaries, we should produce a much more flexible teaching aid. Such a work would be possible now in book form—and how much more possible when electronically-accessed reference works are the norm.

There are many ways in which these types of dictionary could be combined. Starting from a monolingual, L1 equivalents could be inserted at the beginning of each semantic category (sense); the metalanguage or even the definition could be in L1; the fixed phrases could be not only explained and exemplified in L2, but also translated into L1 . . . the list of possibilities is endless. These L1 sections could be gradually reduced in versions of the dictionary for more advanced users (computer-typesetting has made this quite feasible). Or, starting from the bilingual, a number of monolingual features could be introduced: one could, for example, *not* translate phrases exemplifying straightforward use of the headword; the headwords, or better still the semantic categories (senses) of the headword, could be classified from the point of view of frequency, and entries for the less frequent items could contain a higher proportion of monolingual material. Whole monolingual sections could be included—for example, a survey of functional grammar in L2. Such a hybrid dictionary could conceivably bridge the present gulf between the bilingual and the monolingual.

In the words of Dr. Johnson: "In lexicography, as in other arts, naked science is too delicate for the purposes of life. The value of a work must be estimated by its use: It is not enough that a dictionary delights the critic, unless at the same time it instructs the learner; as it is to little purpose, that an engine amuses the philosopher by the subtilty of its mechanism, if it requires so much knowledge in its application, as to be of no advantage to the common workman" (SJ:1747).

"The value of a work must be estimated by its use"—what are we asking a dictionary to do for the learner? It is not a front-line pedagogical instrument in the same way as a course book, language-lab tape or even a grammar book is. You don't open a dictionary and proceed to learn the language from cold. But a good monolingual must do more than simply convey to the users the meaning of words which they come across in their reading. And a good bilingual is more than just something to take the sweat out of a translation into L1 or L2.

How much, then, is it reasonable to expect of a learners' dictionary? Clearly, it must be accurate in what it includes, and comprehensive within the limits of its original design. The book itself must be legible, and durable, and must fall within the price range of similar works on the market. But that is not enough. A good dictionary must do as much as possible to provide users not only with what they know they want, but with what they don't know they want, as well. A learners' dictionary which offers students an L2 word without telling them how to use it is a dangerous thing in a classroom.

But more than that: a good dictionary must above all be *honest* in its presentation of the facts of the language. Distortion or skewing—for example by presenting facts in a way which a native speaker would be able to use but which might mislead a non-native speaker—must be eschewed, even if the price of clarity is a reduction in the coverage of the book. All lexicographers know the temptation to squeeze the last ounce of information into every line. This often results in an entry so dense as to be incomprehensible, the compiler's last triumphant effort having produced so many hermetic symbols and codes that all the student gets from it is a deep feeling of personal inadequacy.

Therein lies a paradox. Few would disagree with Dr. Johnson's heartfelt cry: "of all the candidates for literary praise, the unhappy lexicographer holds the lowest place". And yet the result of the lexicographer's labours, once in print, bound and in the hands of the student, is endowed with the numinous quality of Moses' tablets. Generations of dictionary users have humbly cried "Mea culpa" when their struggles to decode the dictionary entry were unsuccessful. Let's get it clear: if students use their dictionary carefully and intelligently, and still make mistakes, then there is nothing wrong with the students. There is a great deal wrong with the dictionary.

There is nothing sacred or awe-inspiring about an ordinary everyday dictionary. It is a tool to be used by people who need to know something about a language. But you can't use it properly unless you learn how it works. Like most lexicographers, I meet many serious and dedicated users who have not discovered half of what the dictionary entry contains for them. This is a chastening experience for both them and me. They go off to read the Introduction (but they won't), and I go off to cut down the content and improve the accessibility of the next dictionary (but regularly gang agley at proof stage).

*   *   *   *   *

Bilingual or monolingual dictionary: which serves the learner best? The discussion merits a book in itself, and I shall leave the last word to Dr. Johnson:

"I hope, that though I should not complete the conquest, I shall at least . . . make it easier for some other adventurer to proceed farther . . .".

References

ALD   *Oxford Advanced Learner's Dictionary of Current English*, Oxford University Press, 1981.
AWR   Read, Allen Walker "Dictionaries", *Encyclopaedia Britannica*, Macropaedia vol. 5, 1974.
CELD   *Collins English Learner's Dictionary*, Collins, 1974.
CGD   *Collins German Dictionary*, Collins, 1980.
CRCFD   *Collins-Robert Concise French Dictionary*, Collins, 1981.
CRFD   *Collins-Robert French Dictionary*, Collins, 1978.
CSID   *Collins-Sansoni Italian Dictionary*, Sansoni, 1981.
CULD   *Chambers Universal Learners' Dictionary*, Chambers, 1980.
GEJD   *Global English-Japanese Dictionary*, Sanseido, 1983.
HSFED   *Harrap's Shorter French English Dictionary*, Harrap, 1982.
JRD   Rey-Debove, J. "Problèmes et méthodes de la lexicographie terminologique". Papers from GIRSTERM-UQAM Colloquium, Montreal.
JW   Whitcut, J. "Usage Notes in Dictionaries" (this volume).
LDOCE   *Longman Dictionary of Contemporary English*, Longman, 1978.
NECD   *New English-Chinese Dictionary*, Joint Publishing Co., Hong Kong, 1975.
NKL   *Natur och Kulturs Lexikon (Svensk-Engelsk-Svenskt)*, Söderström, 1953.
SFBD   Thorndike-Barnhart *Scott, Foresman Beginning Dictionary*, Doubleday, USA, 1976.
SJ   Johnson, S. *The Plan of a Dictionary (1747)*, Scolar Press, 1970.

INNOVATIVE PRACTICES IN FRENCH MONOLINGUAL LEARNERS' DICTIONARIES AS COMPARED WITH THEIR ENGLISH COUNTERPARTS

MARIE-NOËLLE LAMY

University of Salford, Great Britain

At first glance, it is difficult to identify French monolingual learners' dictionaries (henceforth MLDs) as, with two or three notable exceptions, their titles bear no trace of their vocations as dictionaries for foreign learners and they make only passing reference to foreign users in their prefaces. Unlike their English counterparts, which are often intended "primarily for the foreign student", as the *Longman Dictionary of Contemporary English* puts it, the priority for French dictionary publishers is on the native learner, particularly within the context of the French educational system.[1]*

To be sure, all the dictionaries mentioned below claim to be of help to anyone wishing to improve his or her knowledge of French, but it is not always clear whether a given approach was adopted specially for the benefit of the foreign reader, or whether it is the fortuitous result of native-directed pedagogical thinking. However, with the exception of defining phrases,[2] it would be foolish to suppose that foreign learners' interests cannot be met by presentations designed for natives, and this article reviews innovative features regardless of the processes which led to their design.

Three books in particular provide most of the examples in the following discussions. These are *Le Robert méthodique*, *Le Dictionnaire du français contemporain* and *Le Dictionnaire Larousse du français langue étrangère* (henceforth respectively RM, DFC and FLE). Amongst works of greater or lesser central relevance to foreign learners, we can also include encyclopaedic dictionaries, thematic dictionaries, usage books and works specializing in particular features of language structure such as Matoré's *Dictionnaire du vocabulaire essentiel* or CLE's *Dictionnaire des structures fondamentales du français*. A description of these works accompanies the bibliography at the end of the article.

When he/she inspects the reference bookshelves, the non-native learner of French finds a large selection of very different dictionaries, capable between them of fulfilling many different needs, but not particularly homogeneous as a whole. Between the linguistically sophisticated learner as envisaged by RM or DFC, the somewhat school-like approach and very basic skills of FLE's typical user and the varied but ill-defined learning needs answered by "glossies" like

---

* Superscript numbers are to Notes at end of article.

Bordas, Hachette and some of the Larousse dictionaries, there are gaps. You will find yourself in one of these if for instance you happen to be a first-year University student reading French, too advanced for FLE but not knowledgeable enough to get the best out of RM or DFC; or again if you are a foreign businessman with a grounding in French and a need to master business styles and vocabularies.

Although within each publishing house a coherent listing policy has in many cases resulted in "families" of dictionaries with recognizable identities, the void between, say, the Robert "family" and the Larousse "family" can only be filled if teachers and students take a hard look at the available material as a whole and make their conclusions public. This is one of the aims of the present study, and as a constructive move towards identifying what must still be achieved, I shall now examine what has been done so far, particularly where it is innovatory.

An "innovation" is here taken to mean a presentation technique, formal or substantive, hitherto not exploited in French or English MLDs, and concerned with assisting the foreign learner in encoding or decoding situations. Decoding for a non-native speaker has largely been seen as a question of understanding meanings, whereas encoding has been deemed to be primarily dependent on good syntax control. Whether influenced by the development of linguistics and applied linguistics or by the autonomous evolution within lexicographical practice, some sections of the professions involved are now arguing that these notions are no longer adequate. This study proposes to show first how one dictionary has succeeded in maximizing the pedagogical efficacy of its structural properties (FLE); it will then concentrate on two innovative works, one of which teaches French through teaching a linguistic approach (DFC) whilst the other (RM) uses a feature of the French lexicon as the basis for language learning. Finally, I shall review a number of more practical innovations in the areas of visual, typographical and other aids.

For a number of years now, French MLDs have been struggling to break out of the traditional form of the dictionary as an alphabetical list. The segregation of certain types of data into appendixes, tables, diagrams or pictures has been dictated by pedagogical considerations arising out of changes in language-teaching techniques. The simplest arrangement is exemplified by the supplement in, for example, *Le Dictionnaire du français vivant*; this has an appendix on blue paper, possibly inspired from the famous "pages roses" in the early *Petit Larousse*, containing traditional appendix material (conjugations, inhabitants of towns, proverbs, etc.) as well as a more useful error-prevention section with homonymic and paronymic confusing pairs (*saint/seing*) (*barbacane/sarbacane*) and potentially misleading endings (*ils émergent/rayon divergent*). More contentiously, the blue pages also list Swiss, Canadian and Belgian "regionalisms". From the point of view of language production, this can be seen as an advance on alphabetical treatment, but it has been criticized for "ghetto-izing" non-metropolitan varieties.

It is significant that efforts to entice learners away from alphabetical consultation habits have been made as the result of applying the principles of structural linguistics to lexicographical design in France, rather than in Britain where structuralism was not so dominant during the sixties and early seventies.

DFC and RM exemplify this strategy and their authors openly refer the readers to antecedent theoretical work. FLE on the other hand has used a carefully designed system of references for practical pedagogical reasons, i.e. to make sure that every part of the text addresses itself to the "right" reader. But in all three cases, the formal structure of the dictionary is itself a tool for learning.

The best example of this new type of organization is FLE, so let us look at it in some detail: not only does the book come in two volumes (*Niveau I* for beginners and *Niveau II* for slightly more advanced learners) and a separate brochure on how to use the dictionary (Cf. p. 31, below), but within each volume and even each entry, the authors have been careful to distribute the material across separate divisions according to degree of difficulty and type of learning activity.

Each entry is planned so as to provide first a simple definition for the least experienced user, followed by a "commentary" for the more fluent learner. Syntactic information, for instance, is given—partly coded—in the basic entry, but it is also treated fully and discursively in the "commentary" section, and expanded further in the traditional end-of-volume grammar section. For each entry, a maximum of three paragraphs (signalled by letters G for "grammatical", S for "semantic" and L for "lexical") may discuss any other interesting features of the headword. Thus *fil* is followed by a paragraph (G) stating its combinatorial possibilities (it can be followed by adjectives or prepositional phrases so as to yield *fil électrique* or *fil de fer*). In paragraph (S) the learner finds usage notes as well as any synonyms, antonyms and related terms, whilst derivations and compounds are to be found in paragraph (L), where a left-to-right and right-to-left system of arrows shows the difference between "direct" and "non-direct" (or non-alphabetical) derivations (e.g. *courir→coureur* but *jambe←enjamber*).

One of the sharpest distinctions between the English and French MLD traditions relates to the treatment of defining vocabulary. Since West and later Ogden developed the notion of controlling the vocabulary to be used in definitions and grammatical descriptions, English MLD lexicographers have worked towards an ever tighter system of defining terms, where values are, if at all possible, constant, and where *definiens* words are always listed as part of the nomenclature, as well as in a separate index (cf. LDOCE). Overall, French MLDs do not compare favourably, contenting themselves in the best cases to promise "clear and simple definitions" in their introductions. But FLE has tried a variation on the West/LDOCE system, by listing in a separate index all the related lexical material suggested in its entries: synonyms, antonyms, terms belonging to the same field, terms belonging to typical collocations, etc.

The idea is not simply to give the reader a lot of vocabulary, as the job could easily be done by an end-of-entry list, like those in *Le Dictionnaire du français vivant* (20 synonyms for the headword *blessure*). FLE is teaching the user through a systematic search within a given field. Thus the entry *boulanger* refers you not only to the word *boulanger*, but to that section of the Grammatical Annexe which deals with the syntax of sentences about "professions" or "jobs", e.g. *il est (no determiner) boulanger*. This integration of semantic and syntagmatic features is taken further in the case of *pain*, with a development combining semantic, syntagmatic and encyclopaedic information: "*pain = ce mot est non-comptable sauf lorsqu'il désigne une sorte de pain d'environ 800g"* followed by a brief essay on bakery products and names of bread-types for vocabulary enlargement.

It might be said at this point that FLE's uses of encyclopaedic information could be made much more explicit. It would then be easier to recognize that what FLE is doing, in some of its entries, is to tackle the difficult problem of pragmatic knowledge. Consider the example of *montagne*: here the learner finds out that, in a French context, a sentence like *aller à la montagne pour Noël* is very likely to be about winter sports and skiing, and not about geographical configurations. Appropriate decoding can only occur if cultural–pragmatic information of this kind has been received, and a mere definition of *montagne* as, for example, "high ground" is inadequate. In this instance, FLE is functioning as a pragmatic dictionary, but it lacks a distinctive notation for highlighting these items. A. Cowie (1984) has advocated the development of an explicit method for the treatment of pragmatic material in MLDs.[3] The example of FLE shows that the need is present even for relatively non-advanced learners.

To return to the structural properties of FLE, we can say that both its macro- and its micro-structure[4] contribute to turning this dictionary into a complete learning "pack". In some respects, FLE overdoes it and overwhelms the user with distracting material but it is truly innovative in its commitment to a flexible presentation promoting activeness and independence in the learner.

In its introduction, DFC insists that "sentence construction" is one of its priorities. It sees one of its main tasks as that of providing the learner with a "normative grammar" of French. Exemplification and grammatical guidance are therefore more interesting in DFC than is definition. Exemplificatory sentences function not only as implicit complements to the bare definition but also as language-learning devices. For example, under *acte*, the example *il vous suffira de faire acte de présence* is itself defined as (= *de paraître en un lieu en n'y restant que quelques instants*). The examples supply the reader with new and not necessarily understood sentence models in order to trigger further consultation acts (whether this actually works is not proven).

Thorough attention has been paid to grammatical guidance, but the crucial difference from LDOCE is the French reluctance to use coded information (except for numbered cross-references to annexed verb conjugations). Verb complementation and adjective position are explained by discursive in-text paraphrases combining syntactic information with generic semantic indicators: [sujet qqn, qqch (concret)] or [sujet qqch (phénomène, état)]. It could be argued that DFC and LDOCE are trying to systematize information presentation in opposite ways, yet the learner is just as likely to be puzzled by abstract semantic primitives (DFC) as by alphanumeric cross-references and algorithms (LDOCE).

Another of DFC's stated aims is vocabulary building, and this is done most notably through a grouping system. Lexemes are removed from their normal alphabetical order and re-assembled according to morpho-semantic relationships. *Affinage* appears as a sub-entry of *affiner*, *entreprise* I (meaning undertaking in general) is a sub-entry of *entreprendre* (= to undertake), but *entreprise* II (meaning commercial or industrial concern) has an entry to itself.

Entretien, however, being polysemic in exactly the same way as its stem verb *entretenir*, appears once in each of the two *entretenir* entries. All this, it will be readily seen, makes consultation a rather risky procedure, unless the user has native intuitions about lexical connections, which is by definition not likely to be true of our foreign learner. More frustrating still, in order to look up *garde-fou* and *garde-chiourme*, you would have to scan two pages and five entries before spotting them on their separate pages.

The corollary of DFC's grouping policy is separation of the resulting homonyms and their derivatives. Here again, it must be said that this does not always make pedagogical or even consultation sense: a student who encounters *fruit* and its derivative *fruitier*, or *fruit* and its derivative *fructueux*, might well want to see them both in an entry or in a table, since learning about differences is also learning about similarities. This, however, is a logical problem, and DFC cannot be accused of inconsistency: having adopted a structural approach, it makes unwavering use of it, and if there is a case to be made for systematic reunion of homonyms, it is *prima facie* neither more nor less convincing than the opposite position. On balance, the consultation difficulties argue against grouping of entries but the method lends itself extremely well to tabular treatment. DFC's remarkable contribution to monolingual learner's lexicography is its presentation of difficult material (grammatical, semantic and lexical) in tables.

The nomenclature may double as an index of grammatical and metalinguistic terms; a user looking up *classe grammaticale*, *fonction grammaticale*, *il/elle/etc.* or *mon/ton/etc.* will find that these entries refer him or her to tables, essays or combinations of both. One example is the *à/de* table, which sets out the behaviour of two prepositions with a high frequency of occurrence in contemporary French and a notorious reputation among foreign learners for being difficult to memorize. For each semantic component (place, time, etc.) *à* and *de* have a box each, containing discursive information, examples and semi-coded extras to allow for language production. The level of sophistication required of the user is fairly high, but assuming such competence, the presentation is excellent. DFC goes as far as to give "negative" information about parallel structures that do *not* contain these prepositions (although the learner might expect them to).

The tables also deal with lexical fields (months of the year, days of the week, kinship terms, military ranks, etc.), confusing pairs (*an/année*, *matin/matinée* etc.) and even pragmatic subtleties (when is the correct time of day for using *bonjour* or *bonsoir*, a more complicated business than might appear at first!). The tables are perhaps best envisaged as summaries, designed to add the finishing touches to the student's knowledge of French. Their role is to confirm, rather than stimulate. Unlike FLE, which sends the reader looking for exercises etc. throughout the text, DFC does not encourage active learning in this sense: browsing is less likely, as the readers are cross-referred from entry to table, but not from table to entry, and as the tables are, symbolically enough, closed by a black framing line. Nevertheless, DFC's pioneering efforts to integrate the function of a dictionary with that of a grammar book must be recognized.[5] DFC is constructed so as to sensitize the student to linguistic differences and similarities. This is indeed the cornerstone of structural linguistics and only by becoming "fluent" in structural thinking will the advanced learner acquire near-native mastery of the foreign language. In encouraging the student to learn and apply this principle, DFC fulfils its role as a tool for advanced language learning.

In contrast to DFC, the priority for *Le Robert méthodique* is vocabulary acquisition. The morphological approach (also used in DFC) is applied in RM with great thoroughness (because the text was prepared with the help of a computer) and precision (because the authors' linguistic positions are based on theory, specifically Nida's work on morphology[6]).

The chief innovation is in the treatment of bound morphemes: whether they are prefixes, suffixes or roots, they are given full entry status, a definition, a description of their lexical relation to other morphemes and a specimen list of lexemes in which they occur. The method for producing RM involved collecting a corpus of 34 290 words, which were then split into morphemes on the principle that a morpheme must occur in at least two different morphological environments. Thus *confesser* is split into CO(N)-, -FESS- and -ER, since each of the three elements can co-occur with a different neighbour:

CO(N)-	confesser, coincider
-FESS-	confesser, professer
-ER	confesser, aimer

The analysis then goes on to treat PRO- and AM- (implying AIM-) in the same way, and so on until the corpus is exhausted. The method does have limitations. In the RM front matter J. Rey-Debove calls it a slightly "flattened" form of distributional analysis: it is good at telling you why *doute* and *douteux* are connected, but it cannot show the relationship between *doute/douteux* and *indubitable*. But pedagogical considerations, she argues, must come before descriptive complexities in these cases. Similarly, the synchronic rule is sometimes broken if this helps vocabulary acquisition. For example, although *chalum-* and *calum-* do not both qualify as synchronic morphemes according to Nida's principles, they are nevertheless given equal entry rights, under the same entry, in order to show the link between *calumet* and *chalumeau* [Cf. Stein, this volume, p. 38—ed.].

RM's morphological emphasis sometimes also forces it to stretch its wordlist policy: having decided to restrict themselves to everyday vocabulary, RM lexicographers find it necessary to include some very rare scientific terms simply because they contain useful morphemes: thus *stylobate* has to be included because of *acrobate*, and *doryanthe* because of *doryphore*. This can also be justified, according to Rey-Debove, by the stress on vocabulary memorization.

But RM's interest in lexical relations is most usefully translated into a cross-reference system of such refinement that it is almost possible for the advanced learner to use RM as a thesaurus.

Connections between single words and phrases (*rendre l'âme* to *mourir*), bound morphemes and lexemes (*sol(i)-* to *soliloque, soliste* and *solitaire*), morpheme and morpheme (*somn-* to *hypno-*, or *-phob-* to *-phil-*), in relationships of synonymy, antonymy or hyponymy (*rompre* to *interrompre*) are clearly displayed and if used skilfully by the advanced learner can acquaint him or her with an expanding network of new vocabulary. It can also work as an aid to spelling. Take *sinanthrope* versus *cynocéphale*: *sinanthrope* refers to a hominid whose remains were discovered in China, as anyone can see who looks up *sin-* and *anthrop-*, whereas *cynocéphale* comes from *cyno-* and *-céphal-* and refers to a dog-headed baboon. The student might also like to speculate on the difference between *sinanthrope* and *héliotrope*, and then perhaps go on to examine the difference between *-trope* (the morpheme) and *trope* (the word) etc. Similarly, the treatment of homographic morphemes is very effective in RM: it clarifies lexical relations whilst building up vocabulary, e.g. *-man-* meaning *rester* as in *manoir*, *permanent*, is opposed to *-man-* meaning *main* as in *manucure* and *remanier*, and to *-man-* meaning *obséder/obsession* as in *maniaque* and *mégalomane*. Through all these examples it can be seen that the teaching strategy is chosen so as to display the nature of French morphology.

Le Robert méthodique, then, is a superb tool for encouraging creativity and answering complex decoding needs. A learning approach based on RM's lexical families has the added advantage that it can make more intelligible to students the effects used by native speakers in punning, and by native writers in various creative techniques (for instance "literalization", frequently called upon by writers to restore a forgotten literal meaning to a figurative or idiomatic phrase for stylistic impact). An advanced student, a future translator perhaps, surely needs access to this kind of information.

The features I have discussed so far fall into the category of substantive innovations and reflect lexicographers' attitudes to (a) language and (b) language learning. I shall now briefly examine some more formal techniques, i.e. choices that tend to reflect the lexicographer (or the publisher)'s attitude to consultation habits. Recognizing that the best-laid plans for packaging information will misfire if the reader's reference skills are poor[7] recent MLDs have started teaching these in their introduction, and some have even been produced with a companion brochure explaining "how to use this dictionary". The idea is excellent, providing the authors do not lose sight of the requirement that students be taught how to find what they need, not how to reconstruct the lexicographer's routine.[8] Another difficulty with this technique is the need to separate descriptions of dictionary lay-out from production exercises. *Chambers Universal Learners' Workbook*, for instance, has a series of tests designed to check comprehension of the CULD text.[9] FLE's *Comment se servir du dictionnaire*, although it deals with less complex linguistic material, is able to elicit retrieval and production of pragmatic knowledge. The FLE brochure is concerned less with explicating the contents of its companion dictionary than with generating linguistic activity around it. An ideal skills-development document should perhaps contain elements of both approaches, providing they were clearly marked as serving different purposes. Even the most complete exploitation of the separate brochure format to date, OUP's *Use Your Dictionary* (a companion to both ALD and OSDCE) does not make the distinction explicit.[10]

The survey would not be complete without a look at typographical and visual ideas. As their very appearance is a major factor in their success, I have chosen to simply quote the most interesting among them in the table below. Column three describes the linguistic problem being highlighted by each particular visual sign.

Dictionary	Design feature	Linguistic feature
Mots Abstraits Pluriguide Nathan	opération gen / chir / mil	Semantic specialization of terms is clearly shown by right-of-text indentation and grey boxed labels—CELD, CULD and OSDCE use similar devices
Hachette Langue Française	ENCYCL.	signals encyclopaedic, as opposed to linguistic, information
DFC	ivre ↓ gris ↑ saoul	downwards arrow precedes a synonym with a weaker meaning than the headword; upwards arrow precedes a synonym with a stronger meaning than the headword
FLE RM	→ ▼	direct derivations
FLE RM	← ▽	indirect derivations (or non-alphabetically derivable)
RM	divorce COUR.	denotes a non-specialist use of a specialized term. COUR. = courant = everyday
Mots Abstraits Pluriguide Nathan	ATT!	This signals contentious spellings, usage etc. [Cf ALD's ⚠ = taboo—ed.]
Robert Méthodique Micro-Robert	two-tone typography	all headwords are in red in M–R and in brown in RM
DFV	blue pages	contains all non-lexical information, plus proverbs, "regionalisms", confusibles
Bordas Larousse DFC Illustré	good quality photographic illustrations	encyclopaedic information. The effect is very motivating for the user
FLE	CONDUIRE	The cartoons illustrate the semantic concept. But they also contribute to vocabulary building and sentence production: each drawing has a typical sentence associated with it but printed separately from it in the end-of-volume index. Students are encouraged to match them up, and invent new ones to describe the same drawings: "elle conduit beaucoup trop vite, elle va avoir un accident" [Cf. Hill, this volume, p 119—Ed.]
FLV	| arrivage arrivée arriver	brackets together all the members of a lexical family

In conclusion, we can say that although dictionaries like RM and DFC are less geared to the early stages of learning than their English counterparts, they do provide the advanced learner with sophisticated linguistic information. They favour discursiveness and implicit [Cf. Jackson, this volume, "Implicit Grammar"—ed.] treatment of data. These traits may be explained by the fact that the market for the books mentioned in this study is, with the exception of FLE, largely composed of native buyers. I suggest that the preponderance of native-speaker-oriented lexicography is a result of the worldwide dominance of EFL needs over French-as-a-foreign-language needs, except for a growing French-as-a-second-language in Africa (see bibliography). French MLDs thus present a very different profile from their English counterparts, with the bulk of the production being devoted to high-quality descriptive dictionaries, and one isolated example of a radical attempt to integrate pedagogy and lexicography (FLE). However, the language dictionaries of the last two or three years display some signs that awareness of the foreign-learner market has increased, and we may look forward to a confirmation of this trend in the future.

Notes

English monolingual dictionaries of relevance to the present study include:
Chambers Universal Learners' Dictionary, 1980 (CULD).
Collins English Learner's Dictionary, 1977 (CELD).
Longman Dictionary of Contemporary English, 1978 (LDOCE).
Oxford Advanced Learner's Dictionary of Current English, OUP 1981 (ALD).
Oxford Dictionary of Current Idiomatic English, OUP, Vol. I, 1975, Vol. II, 1983 (ODCIE).
Oxford Student's Dictionary of Current English, 1978 (OSDCE).
Longman Dictionary of American English, 1983 (LDAE).

1. As J. Dubois pointed out, this was very much the case until the beginning of the seventies. He was hoping that the trend was about to change. Dubois' article "French Monolingual Dictionaries" was published in *Applied Linguistics*, Vol. II, No. 3, 1981.
2. To gloss *girouette* as "plaque mobile autour d'un axe fixé au sommet d'un édifice et qui indique par son orientation la direction du vent", or *fracture* as "lésion osseuse" is to make the foreign learner pay the price of DFC's catch-all user policy. Indeed, what matters to a non-native trying to understand the value of *girouette* is the criterion of wind-direction finding. *Fracture*, a foreign student should be told, functions as a carrier not only of the denotation "os cassé" but, importantly, of the connotations [accidents, pain]. This could have been accomplished at a stroke with *cassure* or *rupture*, both free from the osteopathic connotation of *lésion osseuse*.
3. Cowie, A. P. "EFL dictionaries: past achievements and present needs" in: *LEXeter '83 Proceedings*, ed. R. R. K. Hartmann, Niemayer: Tübingen, 1984.
4. The macro-structure of a dictionary is defined as the overall organization of the work whereas the micro-structure refers to the type of lay-out used within the entries. [Cf. p. 127].
5. The same emphasis is characteristic of DFC's followers, i.e. *Le Nouveau DFC illustré* and *Larousse Lexis*.
6. Nida, E., *Morphology, the Descriptive Analysis of Words*, University of Michigan, 1946.
7. A refined system such as the syntactic coding in LDOCE and ODCIE (I) may well be too complex for the average user. The recently published second part of ODCIE relies much more on self-explanatory labels and glosses. Similarly, CELD makes occasional use of in-text notes.
   Another example is the laudable attempt, in *Lexique du français pratique* to help learners with the morphological irregularities of some French verb endings. But which learner could guess that this explanation is to be found under *-ayer*, at letter *n*? [Cf. Whitcut, this volume, p. 80—Ed.].
8. In the "Dictionary Skills Workbook" within the *Longman Dictionary of American English*, for example, the learner is asked to slot compound nouns into a partially filled list. The

instructions describe the lexicographers' policy for positioning compounds and the learner is merely set the task of imitating them.

9. Kirkpatrick, E. M., *Chambers Universal Learners' Workbook*, Chambers, 1981.
19. Underhill, A., *Use Your Dictionary*, OUP, 1980.

Bibliography

Dictionnaire de la langue française Lexis, Larousse, 1979
   Follows the same linguistic principles as DFC, but with a much bigger wordlist (76 000 words).

Dictionnaire des difficultés du français (Les Usuels), Robert, 1978
   A usage book, in the classical mould, with essays on various types of problems and a prescriptive answer to them.

Dictionnaire des expressions et locutions figurées (Les Usuels), Robert, 1979
   A dictionary of phrases, with definitions, quotations, datations and discursive essays on diarchronic variants.

Dictionnaire des Mots Abstraits (Pluriguides), Nathan, 1981
   This only lists full lexical words.

Dictionnaire des structures fondamentales du français, CLE, Nathan, 1979
   Deals mainly with grammatical words and treats them in depth within sentence contexts. 567 entries.

Dictionnaire du français fondamental pour l'Afrique, Didier, 1974
   Based on Gougenheim's *Dictionnaire fondamental de la Langue française*, with special emphasis on those phrases which are most useful when communicating in French within Africa. E.g. the polysemy of items like *avocat* and *colonie* is treated with a different emphasis from that usually prevalent in metropolitan French.

Lexique du français pratique, Solar, 1981
   A usage book, integrating encyclopaedic with syntagmatic and spelling information on selected (difficult) words. Lists difficult or unexpected genders together at the beginning of each alphabetical letter. It also discusses other prescriptive dictionaries' opinions, particularly where they clash. For advanced learners only.

Dictionnaire du français vivant, Bordas, 1976
   A good general dictionary (45 000 words). Advice on how to use the dictionary is included in the preface (presented as a series of exercises aimed at getting the reader to "warm up" progressively)—3 columns of text per page and a supplement on blue paper make the text easy to consult. A novel, though perhaps contentious, idea is to list definitions *after* the examples in each entry, to reflect the natural order of "total immersion" language learning.

Dictionnaire du vocabulaire essentiel, Larousse, 1963, Matoré
   Covers the 5000 words "français fondamental" only. For beginners.

Dictionnaire Hachette de la langue française, 1980
   The only dictionary to risk making the difference between encyclopaedic and linguistic information explicit.

Dictionnaire Hachette Junior, 1980
   This is one exception to the native-learner orientation of most beginners' dictionaries: it addresses itself specifically to adolescent foreign learners.

Dictionnaire Larousse du français langue étrangère (*Niveau I* and *Niveau II*), 1979
   This is described in detail in the article. The basic wordlist in Niveau I is 2581 words, but comes to 7700 with the addition of related words (as in the G, S, & L paragraphs). Niveau II has 5000 basic entries, 10 000 including related words.

Duden Français, Dudenverlag, 1962
   A very old classic from the pictorial dictionary publishers. Still useful to the beginner for basic names of objects. [Cf. Hill, this volume, p. 115—Ed.]

Nouveau dictionnaire des difficultés du français moderne, Duculot, 1983
   A usage book for advanced learners, to be used in connection with Grevisse's classic grammar, *Le Bon usage*.

Nouveau dictionnaire du français contemporain illustré, Larousse, 1980
   Based on DFC, with up-to-date encyclopaedic information and illustrations providing a starting point for vocabulary building.

II. PARTS OF DICTIONARIES

WORD-FORMATION IN MODERN ENGLISH DICTIONARIES

GABRIELE STEIN

University of Hamburg, West Germany

A general-purpose language dictionary describes the vocabulary stock of a given language. This lexical stock consists of primary and of secondary elements. Primary elements are linguistic signs in the Saussurean sense of the term, which cannot be analysed further into smaller linguistic signs but which may serve as a basis for secondary items. They typically occur as either free morphemes, e.g. *bake*, *bed*, *powder*, *river*, or bound morphemes, e.g. *-er*, *-ing*, *-logy*, *-y*. Secondary items are then combinations of primary elements, the rules for combining such primary elements varying from language to language. Examples for English are *baker*, *baking powder*, *bedding*, *powdery*, *river bed*, and *philology*. Bound morphemes are generally regarded as being either inflectional or derivational in function. The former are part of the grammar of a language in the traditional sense and the latter part of lexicology, and within this latter field, of word-formation.

A landmark in the history of English word-formation research was the publication of Hans Marchand's book *The Categories and Types of Present-Day English Word-Formation* in the year 1960. Marchard was the first linguist to observe the synchronic principle in English word-formation with scientific consistency. The field of word-formation was defined by him as follows (Marchand, 1969:2):

> Word-formation is that branch of the science of language which studies the patterns on which a language forms new lexical units, i.e. words. Word-formation can only be concerned with composites which are analysable both formally and semantically. . . .

For Marchand the word-formative patterns comprise the following processes, all regarded as constituting one group: compounding, prefixation, suffixation, derivation by a zero-morpheme, and backderivation. Words of this group are "formed as grammatical syntagmas, i.e. combinations of full linguistic signs" (Marchand, 1969:2). A second group is characterized as "words which are not grammatical syntagmas, i.e. which are composites not made up of full linguistic signs" (Marchand, 1969:2) and the processes which belong to this group are expressive symbolism, blending, clipping, rime and ablaut gemination, and word-manufacturing. The common feature of both groups is "that a

new coining is based on a synchronic relationship between morphemes"
(Marchand, 1969:3).

For the first group, which will be in the centre of my discussion, this means
that full compounds must be opposable to either free morpheme, e.g. *river bed*
to *river* and *bed*, and derivatives must be opposable to their underived basis and
to other derivatives containing the same bound morpheme, e.g. *baker* to *bake*
and *driver*, *smoker*.

Word-formation studies on English in the decades following the publication
of Hans Marchand's standard work have basically focussed on the following
aspects:

1. the place of word-formation within a specific theoretical frame-work and
    the implications for the latter;
2. the further elaboration of word-formation rules with respect to phono-
    logical, syntactic, and semantic constraints;
3. specific word-formation processes or affixes on the basis of empirical
    data;
4. the psycholinguistic, sociolinguistic, and pragmalinguistic components in
    English word-formation in the wake of the recent development of these
    linguistic fields.

The question of the functional unity of word-formation itself (that is, the
question of whether all word-forming processes have actually been subsumed
under the field of word-formation), and the question of what the functional
units of word-formation are, have both been given less attention. Yet if
changes of the syntactic-semantic class of a word, e.g.

intransitive verb ⟶	transitive verb
He *ran*.	He *ran* the water.
uncountable noun ⟶	countable noun
He bought some *coffee*.	He ordered two *coffees*.

are also included under word-formation (cf. Quirk *et al.*, 1972: 1015–1017;
Stein, 1977b: 229 ff), the change does not result in a new word but in an
additional syntactic–semantic property of the word in question. Similar
considerations hold for purely semantic changes of the type:

noun denoting container ⟶	noun denoting content of the container
a milk *bottle*	two *bottles* of milk

where the item, a *bottle*, has acquired a further sense. Both types of
phenomena, if regarded as constituting part of word-formation, challenge the
basic concept of word-formation itself, that of the word. Is it a new word that
has been coined? If the answer to this question is negative, a definition of
word-formation like Marchand's can no longer be maintained. The whole field
will have to be redefined. The other challenge to the widely accepted view of
word-formation outlined above comes from new formations with combining
forms, e.g. *Euro-*+*-crat*.

Once formations of this type become productive in modern English,
combinations consisting of a bound morpheme+a bound morpheme,

excluded in Marchand's theory of word-formation on a native basis of coining, will have to become an integral part of English word-formation. Since combining forms are only just attracting scholars' attention the term itself is not entirely clear in word-formation research (cf. in this respect Adams, 1973; Stein, 1977a; Bauer, 1979, 1983).

On the basis of this admittedly very brief summary of the state of research on modern English word-formation I shall discuss the treatment of affixes (here taken to include combining forms as well as prefixes and suffixes), word-formation processes, and word-formation products in some modern English dictionaries. In order to capture as much variety of lexicographical practice as possible the present study is based on the latest works of five different publishing houses on both sides of the Atlantic. The publishers are: Chambers, Collins, Longman, Oxford University Press, and Merriam-Webster. The dictionaries in question are all modern English monolingual desk dictionaries. With respect to the envisaged user two groups have to be distinguished: the group of dictionaries for the native language user includes *Chambers Twentieth Century Dictionary*, *Collins English Dictionary* (CED), *The Concise Oxford Dictionary of Current English* (COD), the *Longman New Universal Dictionary* (LNUD), and *Webster's Ninth New Collegiate Dictionary* (W9); the group of dictionaries aimed at the foreign learner includes *Chambers Universal Learners' Dictionary* (CULD), the *Oxford Advanced Learner's Dictionary of Current English* (ALD), and the *Longman Dictionary of Contemporary English* (LDOCE). My reason for choosing desk dictionaries rather than unabridged ones is that the former call for a well-argued vocabulary selection out of the total stock of items available and that this selection is partially based on the internal structure of the items themselves. Dictionaries for the foreign learner are included in order to bring out the contrast between the decoding and the encoding aspect in word-formation.

I shall concentrate on two issues: 1. Are there specific lexicographical problems of word-formation; that is, are there aspects of word-formation that are peculiar to, created by, the form of the dictionary itself, and if so, which are they?

2. What is the relation between modern English word-formation research and modern English lexicography? Is there any relation at all, and if so, is this influence unilateral or bilateral?

1. Lexicographical Problems of Word-formation

For all word-formations we have to distinguish the linguistic elements used, the processes of formation, and the results or products of this formation. The choice of items to be included in a particular dictionary and their presentation within it constitute problems for the practical lexicographer. The choice of items concerns the formative elements—whether free or bound—as well as the resulting formations. It obviously depends on the overall policy of the dictionary editors. Affixes may be expected to be given a relatively extensive coverage in desk dictionaries because of their great decoding value. This does indeed hold for the dictionaries under discussion aimed at the native speaker.

Affixes are generally treated as headwords in the A–Z text and the basic, still productive core is listed. The three dictionaries for the foreign learner show three different policies. The LDOCE, not exclusively geared towards the non-native user, lists them as main entries in the A–Z text as the native-speaker dictionaries do. CULD has adopted a rather peculiar but consistent policy: it lists most of the linguistic elements that are traditionally regarded as combining forms in the A–Z text, but prefixes and suffixes go into an appendix. The ALD lists most of the combining forms and some prefixes and suffixes in the A–Z text, and the appendix after irregular verbs and abbreviations lists some combining forms and most of the prefixes and suffixes. ALD's and CULD's treatment comes rather as a surprise. Affixes are, it is true, given a specific section in the dictionary, but it is a supplementary one and suggests to me that their word-analysing property has been underrated. In dictionaries for the foreign learner there is generally a stronger emphasis on the encoding language needs of the learner. ALD's and CULD's policy is all the more astonishing because affixes have a high word-generating potential for the encoding user. The reason for ALD's and CULD's rather contradictory position is to be sought in their word-formation analyses: in both dictionaries the synchronic principle is not recognized. As long as this principle is not observed, however, there is no way of dealing successfully with the productive aspect of word-formation. An entry like

   ab-   /æb-, əb-/ *pref* from, away from: *absent*; *abduct*. (ALD)

for instance, makes it impossible for the user to generate new *ab-* items: *-sent* and *-duct* cannot be recognized as linguistic signs with the remainder of the meaning in present-day English. The user will therefore not generate new *ab-* derivatives. All he might do is to interpret the first syllable of *ab-*words as meaning 'from, away from'. The ability to make such interpretations is, of course, important in understanding the etymologies of those dictionaries that provide them, but is of less immediate relevance in those (e.g. learners' dictionaries) that do not (Cf. Ilson, 1983) [also Cf. Lamy, this volume, p. 30—ed.].

Suffix combinations too, are occasionally listed, either as headwords or as run-on entries, e.g. *ably* ⟨ -*able* + -*ly*, -*ally* ⟨ -*al* + -*ly*, etc. They are, however, not called suffix combinations but suffixes which, strictly speaking, would only hold for those cases in which the form is one functional-semantic unit, e.g. -*ally* as an adverbializer for adjectives in -*ic* that have no -*ical* variant: *terrific*→*terrifically*. -*Ably* as a synchronic affix can only be regarded as a suffix combination of -*able* + -*ly*, as in *reliably*. Adverbs in -*ably* are not formed directly from verbs or nouns without the intermediate stage of an adjective in -*able*.

As to the inclusion of open compounds (those not written as one word) as dictionary entries, and of derivatives as dictionary entries with explanations (rather than as undefined run-ons or items listed to exemplify prefixes), lexicographers usually take into account their internal semantic structure. The more the meaning of a combination is assumed to be inferrable from the meaning of its constituents listed in the dictionary and the process of formation itself, the stronger the likelihood that it will not be listed as a dictionary item.

The criterion of word transparency is usually mentioned in the preface to the dictionary but it is never defined. The only dictionary editor who has tried to define transparency is P. B. Gove (Gove, 1966; Stein, 1976, 1984). So far neither lexicographers nor linguists have been able to give a satisfactory definition of the term, which accounts for the fact that dictionaries, although applying the same criterion, vary greatly with respect to the self-explanatory word-formations omitted.

The editors' views on word-formation are also reflected in the way in which affixes and word-formation products (compounds and derivatives) are presented in their dictionaries. Forms of presentation are thus intricately tied up with our second issue, the interdependence between word-formation research and lexicography. Problems of presentation may concern both affixes and actual word-formations. As morphemes, affixes should be given the same lexicographical treatment as all other morphemes and morpheme combinations in the dictionary. Because of their word-generating potential, however, their presentation will necessarily have to be different. A close study of the dictionaries under review reveals that, in general, both these requirements are not yet met, though there is a noticeable tendency towards greater explicitness, found above all in LDOCE.

Spelling variants of the type *haemo-*, *hemo-*; *-ize*, *-ise* are usually listed. The indication of pronunciation is not yet universal practice. For prefixes and suffixes it could unambiguously be given. Dictionaries that are deficient in this respect are usually also unaware of the synchronic principle in word-formation. Combining forms are a special case. When they are combined with another constituent their phonological shape may change, e.g. *necro-* in combination with *-phobia* and *-tomy*: *necrophobia* [ˌnekrə ˈfəʊbɪə], *necrotomy* [neˈkrɒtəmɪ].

Restrictive usage labels are not as consistently applied as in other lexical items. Combining forms, for instance, which are mostly productive in technical or scientific use are not always given subject field labels such as *Chem.*, *Phys.*, etc.

Affix definitions, as is well illustrated by Dwight Bolinger's paper in this volume, are usually extremely brief and therefore often unsatisfactory. They may even occasionally be misleading as is evidenced by COD's description of *arch-*:

> **arch-** *pref.* w. sense (1) chief, superior, (arch*bishop*, arch*diocese*, arch*duke*), (2) preeminent, esp. extremely bad, (arch*fiend*) . . .

The definition would not prevent the user from coining such words as **archcivil servant*, **archofficer*, **archteacher* for sense (1) and such words as **archmother*, **archwriter*, **archstudent* for sense (2). What one misses are collocation restrictions with respect to the semantic classes of nouns that can be combined with the prefix *arch-*. For other lexical items such collocation specifications are common lexicographical practice, e.g. *blond* . . . (of hair) light-coloured; *bounce* . . . (of a ball) to spring back or up again from the ground.

The widespread unsatisfactory lexicographical treatment of homographs is in general extended to homographic affixes. One of the deficiencies is the predominantly diachronic approach in synchronic dictionaries, the application of the etymological criterion in those cases where synchronic criteria are required. Items that are etymologically related are treated together, those that have different etymologies are regarded as different items. In the case of affixes, as elsewhere, this etymological principle often overrides functional and semantic aspects. One has the impression that affixes of the same form are indiscriminately lumped together. The LNUD, for instance, has the following entry for -*ade*:

> **-ade**   /-ayd/ *suffix* (————→*n*) **1a** act or action of ⟨*block*ade⟩ ⟨*escap*ade⟩ **b** individual or group of people involved in (a specified action) ⟨*cavalc*ade⟩ ⟨*reneg*ade⟩ **2** product; *esp* sweet drink made from (a specified fruit) ⟨*lime*ade⟩

The examples for sense 1b *cavalcade* and *renegade* cannot be regarded as derivatives from a synchronic point of view, there are no morphemes *cavalc-*, *reneg-*. The existence of a suffix -*ade* with sense 1b is thus rather doubtful. The deverbal noun suffix -*ade* (sense 1a) and the denominal noun suffix -*ade* (sense 2) are semantically totally unrelated and therefore a homographic treatment ¹-*ade* and ²-*ade* would have been more appropriate.

The example quoted also illustrates two features which are affix-specific forms of presentation in a dictionary. The observation of the synchronic principle in word-formation enables the lexicographer to specify the grammatical properties of affixes. He can not only indicate the parts of speech with which a particular affix combines (and with which meaning), but also the grammatical function or functions of that affix. The word-generating, dynamic property of affixes is so far handled best in LDOCE as can be seen from the following example which also contains the second feature of presentation, the listing of examples to illustrate the type of formation in question:

> **-ate**   /¹₂T, EIt/ *suffix* **1** [*n* ————→*adj*] full of: *very* AFFECTIONATE **2** [*n* ————→*n*] the total group of people holding (the stated rank or office): *the* ELECTORATE **3** [*n*, *adj* ————→ *v*] to act as; cause to become: *to* ACTIVATE **4** [*n* ————→*n*] *tech* a chemical salt formed from (the stated acid): PHOSPHATE

LDOCE uses the arrow, [*n*————→*adj*], to symbolize word-formation processes. The explicit recording of these processes makes them available for the active language user. It is interesting to note that it is a dictionary not exclusively, but predominantly written for the foreign learner that shows this form of presentation. It thus supports the encoding aspect of the dictionary. LNUD, another dictionary of the Longman Group, uses the arrow too—thus deviating from the 8th edition of *Webster's New Collegiate Dictionary* (W8) from which it is obviously derived according to the word-formation analyses and examples listed—but it does not generally indicate the bases of formation, that is, the left side of the arrow is often empty: ————→*n*. This practice corresponds more to what might be called the analytic dictionary treatment of word-formation. Suffixes are listed with a part of speech label as if identified as final elements in actually occurring formations. The analytic approach is particularly striking for W8 and W9, other dictionaries are more inconsistent than LDOCE and W9, mixing both approaches rather arbitrarily.

Let us now turn from affixes to word-formation products. There are four basic areas where the presentation of word-formations may cause problems: the distinction between main and run-on entries, the listing of words derived by means of a zero-morpheme, the recording of spelling variants for compounds, and the definition and definition pattern of compounds and derivatives.

The distinction between main entries and run-on entries is usually based on the criterion of lexicalization or the inverse linguistic phenomenon of word transparency. The problematic character of this distinction has already been mentioned above and for the lexicographical problems raised by this distinction, e.g. the observation of the alphabetical principle, the listing of suffixal alternants, etc., the reader is referred to Gove 1966; Stein 1976, 1977a, 1977b, 1979.

With respect to the recording of words derived by means of a zero-morpheme there is much inconsistency in the dictionaries under review. Apart from practical inconsistencies we encounter an internal one: some dictionaries which do not generally use historical ordering for senses nevertheless invoke the historical principle for homographs, including the order in which zero-derivatives are listed. The criteria set up by Marchand (Marchand, 1963, 1969a) to establish the synchronic relationship between such items are thus evidently not applied. It looks as if the editors are not even aware of them. An arbitrary preference for a specific printing style accounts in addition for an unsatisfactory treatment of zero-derivatives from phrasal verbs. The LNUD, for instance, describes its policy as follows (xvii):

> A compound written as a single word comes before the same compound written with a hyphen, which in turn comes before the same compound written as two or more separate words:
> **rundown** *n*
> **run-down** *adj*
> **run down** *vt*

This means that the verb from which the noun and the adjective are derived comes last. The definition of the noun and the adjective will have to anticipate that of the verb. There is no theoretical justification for observing and at the same time disregarding synchronic relationship for zero-derivatives.

With respect to spelling, compounds pose certain lexicographical problems. For primary words spelling variants are usually recorded. For compounds the situation is more complicated. Since the spelling of many compound words in English is not fixed, lexicographers have to decide which spelling of a particular compound their dictionary is to record. Corpus and frequency data are not always available. There seems to be an understanding among English lexicographers that they will never list all three spellings—solid, hyphenated, separate words—of a compound even if actually occurring in the language. Usually only one spelling is given. A close study of the dictionaries under consideration reveals that publishing houses often have a preference for one specific style used when the spelling is not fixed.

An analysis of the definitions given for compounds and derivatives shows that there are two difficulties. Non-lexicalized derivatives (e.g. those with no specialized meanings) of the same type and pattern, e.g. *-ish* derivatives from adjectives designating a colour, are not always defined in the same way (see Stein 1976). This means that the derivational and semantic pattern is not always consistently reflected in actual definitions. This type of internal inconsistency may be due to the internal organization of work, different letters being defined by different lexicographers, or to the endeavour not to use the wording encountered in another dictionary for that very definition. The other difficulty arises in all those cases in which a secondary word has two or more senses of which one is self-explanatory. Editors of desk dictionaries wonder whether they should treat these items like all other lexical items, that is, list them with all their senses, or whether they can omit the self-explanatory sense which usually constitutes the general meaning of the compound or derivative in question. Practice varies. LNUD, for instance, has adopted the following policy (xvii):

> Some words formed with beginnings and endings have a specific meaning, but also a very general one that can be guessed. For these words, the general meaning is shown in the form of an etymology:
> **airer** . . . *n* . . . a free standing, usu collapsible, framework for airing or drying clothes, linen, etc [²AIR + ²-ER]
> This means that the noun **airer** has also a very general meaning which is the sum of the meanings of the verb **air** and the ending **-er**: 'a person or thing that airs' . . .

2. The Relation Between Word-formation Research and Lexicography

From the foregoing discussion it will already have become clear that the influence of word-formation research on modern English lexicography has not been a very profound one. This does not come as too much of a surprise because progress in linguistics on the whole has taken considerable time to make itself felt in lexicography. One of the landmarks in this respect was *Webster's Third New International Dictionary* in which descriptivism, the tenet of modern linguistics, became the overriding principle. Grammatical theory has so far been most deeply absorbed in LDOCE.

As to word-formation, it has to be stressed that the progress made in linguistic research, the setting-up of the synchronic principle and the elaboration of quite a number of formal, functional and semantic rules in word-formation is not yet generally reflected in the lexicographical treatment of word-formation. In addition, dictionaries are not very explicit on the productivity of word-formation processes. Productivity, it is true, is not easy to measure, but it is more fully covered in word-formation research than in lexicography.

An area where research findings become more and more traceable is that of pronunciation. Stress in compounds may shift in certain syntactic constellations and dictionaries are beginning to record such stress shifts. LDOCE, for instance, has a specific mark to signal stress shift: ◄. The use of this mark is explained as follows (xviii) [Cf. Wells, this volume, pp. 48–49—ed.]:

> A number of compounds may have a SHIFT (= "movement") in STRESS when they are used before nouns. For example, *plate glass* would have the pattern /ˌ . ' . / when spoken by

itself, or in a sentence like *The window was made of plate glass*. But the phrase *plate glass window* would usually have the pattern /, . . ' . . /—that is, with the main STRESS of the whole phrase on *window*; *glass* loses most STRESS completely. The syllable with most STRESS in *plate glass* is now *plate*—but it has only SECONDARY STRESS in the phrase as a whole. The mark /   ◄/ is used after words where this happens. For example:
plate glass /ˌ.'.◄/

That linguistic research will and has to influence the making of language dictionaries is self-evident. What is, however, more astonishing is that linguists expect lexicography to incorporate their findings, yet they rarely assume that lexicography might further certain areas of linguistics itself. They use the wealth of linguistic information that dictionaries provide, they rely on lexicographical data. They draw heavily upon these data banks to support or corroborate their theoretical views and therefore regard dictionary information as useful or necessary but of only secondary importance to their theoretical assumptions. They underrate the idea-provoking, insight-providing value of these data because the underlying theoretical framework may not be as coherent or stringent as they think it should or could be. To my mind, however, this insight-providing aspect of lexicographical information cannot be emphasized enough.

For word-formation research the dictionaries under review supply very valuable information on two aspects of word-formation that have not yet received adequate scholarly attention. *First*, most of the dictionaries in question not only distinguish between prefixes and suffixes but include a third type of bound morpheme, combining forms. The definitions given for this term differ and so do the units subsumed under it. We can, however, single out three types of linguistic elements that are regarded as combining forms: linguistic elements of Greek or Latin origin that typically occur with each other, e.g. *bio-*, *geo-*, *-graphy*, *-logy* as in *biography*, *biology*, *geography*, *geology*; forms in *-o-* corresponding to modern English adjectives or nouns, e.g. *Russo-* corresponding to *Russian*; and forms consisting of a free morpheme followed by a bound morpheme which is either *-ed*, *-er* or *-ing*. Examples are *-bodied*, *-breaker*, *-bathing*. What is needed is a well-argued theoretical distinction between these elements, prefixes and suffixes.

The dictionary treatment of combining forms seems to me to be the result of the common lexicographical approach towards language, language analysis rather than language production. The same holds for the *second* aspect of word-formation: dictionaries tend to indicate whether a free morpheme is typically used in combination and as which part of the combination. LDOCE, for instance, has the following entry for *bed*:

bed . . . 3 [C] (*often in comb.*) a piece of ground prepared for plants: *a flowerbed* . . .

and CED specifies that the noun *blackberry* is also used in front of a noun:

blackberry . . . **2. b.** (*as modifier*): *blackberry jam*

A study of present-day English dictionaries seems to suggest that items that function as modifiers in a compound get more emphasis than those that function as a head. This rather arbitrary treatment may be due to the fact that the first part of a word is usually given more attention because of the alphabetical principle. The type of linguistic element that usually occurs with a specific meaning in combinations only, e.g. *bed* as a head with the meaning it has in the combination *flowerbed*, needs more thorough investigation. If such linguistic elements are set up as a word-formation class its relation to the other three units, prefixes, suffixes, and combining forms, will have to be made clear.

References

Adams, V., *An Introduction to Modern English Word-Formation*. Longman, 1973.

Bauer, L., "Against Word-Based Morphology" in *Linguistic Inquiry* **10**: 508–509, 1979.

Bauer, L., *English Word-Formation*. Cambridge University Press, 1983.

Gove, P. B. (ed.), *Webster's Third New International Dictionary*. G. & C. Merriam, 1961.

Gove, P. B., "Self-Explanatory Words" in *American Speech* **41**: 182–198, 1966.

Hanks, P. (ed.), *Collins English Dictionary*. Collins, 1979.

Hornby, A. S., *Oxford Advanced Learner's Dictionary of Current English*. Oxford University Press, 4th edition, 1980.

Ilson, R., "Etymological Information: Can It Help Our Students?" in *ELT Journal* **37**: 76–82, 1983.

Kirkpatrick, E. M. (ed.), *Chambers Universal Learners' Dictionary*. Chambers, 1980.

Kirkpatrick, E. M. (ed.), *Chambers Twentieth Century Dictionary*. Chambers, 1983.

Marchand, H., *The Categories and Types of Present-Day English Word-Formation*. Harrassowitz, 1960; 2nd completely revised and enlarged edition, Beck, 1969.

Marchand, H., "On a Question of Contrary Analysis with Derivationally Connected but Morphologically Uncharacterized Words" in *English Studies* **44**: 176–187, 1963.

Marchand, H., "A Set of Criteria for the Establishing of Derivational Relationship Between Words Unmarked by Derivational Morphemes" in *Indogermanische Forschungen* **69**: 10–19, 1969a.

Mish, F. (ed.), *Webster's Ninth New Collegiate Dictionary*. Merriam-Webster, 1983.

Procter, P. (ed.), *Longman Dictionary of Contemporary English*. Longman, 1978.

Procter, P. (ed.), *Longman New Universal Dictionary*. Longman, 1982.

Quirk, R. *et al.*, *A Grammar of Contemporary English*. Longman, 1972.

Stein, G., "On Some Deficiencies in English Dictionaries" in *Anglo-American Forum* **5**: 1–27, 1976.

Stein, G., "English Combining Forms" in *Linguistica* **9**: 140–147, 1977a.

Stein, G., "The Place of Word-Formation in Linguistic Description" in *Perspektiven der Wortbildungsforschung*. Bouvier, 1977b.

Stein, G., "The Best of British and American Lexicography" in *Dictionaries* **1**: 1–23, 1979.

Stein, G., "Towards a Theory of Lexicography: Principles and/vs Practice in Modern English Dictionaries", in: *Exeter '83 Proceedings*, ed. R. R. Hartmann, Niemayer: Tübingen, 1984.

Sykes, J. B. (ed.), *The Concise Oxford Dictionary of Current English*. Oxford University Press, 1982.

Woolf, H. B. (ed.), *Webster's New Collegiate Dictionary*. G. & C. Merriam, 8th edition, 1973.

ENGLISH PRONUNCIATION AND ITS DICTIONARY REPRESENTATION

J. C. WELLS

Department of Phonetics and Linguistics, University College, London

Not all dictionaries include information about pronunciation. There is little need for such information in a dictionary of Spanish or Finnish, for example, since in all except the rarest of cases the pronunciation of a word in those languages may be safely inferred from its spelling, given knowledge of the relevant "reading rules" which express the relationship between phoneme and grapheme, speech and writing. It is well known, though, that English is not such a language: accordingly, all save the smallest English dictionaries include some form of pronunciation guide, whether in IPA phonetic symbols, in some usually ad-hoc respelling system, or through diacritics attached to the ordinary spelling.

The purpose served by pronunciation indication is much the same in monolingual as in bilingual dictionaries: to advise the user who is unsure of the spoken form of a word by recommending a suitable pronunciation for it. The larger monolingual dictionaries may also nod in the direction of registering the whole range of pronunciation variants currently in use (particularly among educated speakers), although most dictionaries remain firmly prescriptive rather than descriptive. The scholarly specialist pronouncing dictionaries constitute a special case, since they do attempt to cover a range of variants: but even Jones (1977) (hereinafter referred to as *EPD*) for British English and Kenyon and Knott (1953) for American English could not be called comprehensive or indeed objective in the way Martinet and Walter (1973) is for French.

A lexicographer engaged in the compilation of an English dictionary has to make several fundamental decisions about the way pronunciation is to be represented in it. In particular, he must decide what type or types of pronunciation are to be shown; what range of variants is to be included; and what notation system is to be used. Although these questions are not wholly independent of one another, it will be convenient to discuss them in that order.

1. Types of pronunciation

Dictionaries published in Britain usually prescribe as their model accent, whether explicitly or implicitly, British Received Pronunciation (RP: for discussion of this concept see, for example, the Introduction to *EPD* and Wells, 1982: 117–118, 279–301). Uniformity on this point is slightly reduced by the fact that dictionaries in the Oxford tradition, owing perhaps to a combination

45

of historical emphasis and a Scottish influence in their authorship, have shown certain phonemic contrasts long obsolete in RP (though present in some varieties of American English), such as the distinction between the vowels of *horse* and *hoarse*, *short* and *sport* (a contrast allowed for even by Chambers, 1983). EFL-oriented dictionaries which emanate from Britain or from countries where a British model of English is customarily taught are unanimous for RP, and have tended to be based very firmly upon *EPD* and the Daniel Jones tradition (something which is not the case with dictionaries aimed at the native-speaker market).

Dictionaries published in the United States eschew RP as something extraneous to American usage and base their pronunciation indications on "General American", meaning an American pronunciation lacking any noticeable Eastern or Southern characteristics. (American dialectologists deny the scholarly validity of this concept, but it clearly has its uses in lexicography and the teaching of English as a second or foreign language.)

There are also dictionaries available which take Australian (Macquarie 1981) or Indian English (Nihalani *et al.* 1979) as their pronunciation norm.

For EFL purposes, in particular, there is a good case for reflecting both major pronunciation norms in a bilingual dictionary, with double pronunciation entries wherever RP and General American diverge. An important pioneer in this direction is LDOCE, 1978. For one recent major monolingual dictionary (GID, 1984) the present writer contributed pronunciation entries aiming to reflect a wide range of educated accents of English (although the decision of the publishers not to include any detailed explanation of the symbolizations and conventions applied somewhat reduced the usefulness of this attempt).

The lexicographer's task is lightened in this respect by the fact that many differences between accents (pronunciation varieties) are matters of mere phonetic realization, such that a single pronunciation entry can stand equally for all. The various qualities of vowel-sound that people use in the word *face* can all be represented by the same symbol (whether as IPA /feɪs/, respelling *fayss*, or diacritical *fās*). Australian, Scottish, and Old Etonian users can each interpret the transcription in accordance with their own pronunciation habits, and nothing is lost.

Nothing is lost, that is, as long as the accents in question share the same phoneme system (inventory) and the same phonotactic constraints. Those with a smaller phoneme system than that assumed by the transcriber can merely ignore some of his distinctions (as most of us ignore the non-rhyme implied by Chambers' transcriptions of *short* and *sport* with different vowel symbols); but those with a larger one are left with no guidance. Those who use a longer vowel in *bad* and *mad* than in *pad* and *lad* (Wells 1982: 288–289) are given no advice by dictionaries on which length of vowel to use in *ad* or *shad*. The many Scots who make a sharp distinction in pronunciation between pairs such as *tide* and *tied* (Wells 1982: 405–406) have to forgo the lexicographer's aid in making up their minds about the controversial cases *knives* and *python*. A more important case, perhaps, is that of the vowels in *toe* and *told*. Many English people, including many whose speech is very close to RP as traditionally described, and no doubt including many teachers of EFL, have the intuition that these are "different sounds" (technically, that is, realizations not of the same phoneme but of different phonemes). It is easily shown that the special quality of diphthong used by such speakers in *told* occurs in all words where traditional RP has the *toe* vowel followed within the same syllable by /l/, so that the distribution with [əʊ] in *toe, soap, own* but [ɒʊ] in *told, roll*, is predictable and hence not distinctive and not deserving of separate symbolization in a phonemic transcription; yet the operation of tendencies towards morphological regularization and uncertainties about syllable boundaries can lead to non-rhymes in *polar* vs. *roller, slowly* vs. *goalie*, so tending to justify the feeling that for some speakers we ought to recognize a phoneme /ɒʊ/ alongside /əʊ/. Foreign learners, though, can perfectly well ignore the distinction (in the company of speakers of traditional RP).

In fact, most of the anguishing which consciencious lexicographers and phoneticians may undergo in connection with the selection and definition of RP as a British English pronunciation standard are of little relevance to the needs of the EFL learner, precisely because most of the subtle details by which native speakers recognize the social and geographical affiliation of other educated Englishmen are matters of phonetic realization which do not affect the phonemic system involved. (It is this fact which underles Trim's argument (1961) for an "English Standard Pronunciation".)

2. Range of variants shown

The dictionary user who is in search of pronunciation advice will usually be most satisfied if he is offered just a single recommendation for each word. Unfortunately, though, in real life many English words exhibit a multiplicity of spoken forms even within the single accent RP.

At one level there is nothing to be done about this except for the exercise of lexicographical judgement. In ELT it may be sensible to prescribe that *either* be /ˈaɪðə/, *ate* /et/, *again* /əˈgen/, and *often* /ˈɒfn/. But it would be a dull learner who, on exposure to native speakers, failed to notice the frequency with which the alternative forms /ˈiːðə/, /eɪt/, /əˈgeɪn/, /ˈɒftən/ are to be heard; and he may well feel that these latter forms, being the ones which correspond more closely to the usual spelling conventions, might well be the ones which should have been recommended (even though RP speakers may consider them not quite so pukka as the former ones).

These words are nevertheless exceptional in that the existence of their variant pronunciations is unpredictable, not part of any general pattern. The more usual tendency is for variant pronunciations to follow regular and statable rules. In such cases it is possible to take for granted that the native speaker knows the rules, so that the variant need not be mentioned; but in ELT one is faced with the choice between teaching the rule (so that again the variants need no mention) and listing the variants at each entry (leaving the rule to be inferred or ignored).

The best-known example is perhaps that of words ending (in RP and similar accents) with /ə/ or one of certain other vowels, which attracts a following /r/

when followed in connected speech by a word beginning with a vowel: thus *letter* /'letə/, but *letter of credit* /'letər əv 'kredɪt/, *far below* /'fɑː bɪ'ləʊ/ but *far away* /'fɑːr ə'weɪ/. *EPD* uses the special convention here of writing an asterisk to "indicate a possible *r*-link before a following vowel", thus /'letə*/, /fɑː*/, and this essentially ad-hoc convention has been followed by several bilingual dictionaries. In real life, however, an *r*-link is just as likely to occur with words such as *comma*, *Shah* (where there is no orthographic *r* and *EPD* therefore writes no *), and I cannot help feeling it would be better to drill learners in the use of /r/ to prevent hiatus after any non-close vowel and forget about putting asterisks in dictionary entries. The principle involved is after all the same as the one which causes *feared* to be pronounced /fɪəd/ but *fearing* /'fɪərɪŋ/, the first with and the second without a phonetically realized /r/. This principle can be expressed as a "phonological rule" to the effect that an /r/ can always be inserted (and within a word usually must be inserted) if a vowel sound follows immediately after one of /ə ɪə eə ʊə ɜː ɑː ɔː/.

There are many other familiar examples of phonological rules, often optional, which generate pronunciation variants for whole classes of words. The syllabic consonant rule specifies a tendency towards a one-segment syllabic [n̩] after a single obstruent, as in *garden*, *listen*, but a two-segment vowel-plus-consonant sequence [ən] after anything else, as in *common*, *sullen*, *lion*: but that is not to imply that people don't also say ['gɑːdən] alongside ['gɑːdn̩]. Between a single consonant and an unstressed vowel there is frequently alternation between /iː/, /ɪ/ and the semivowel /j/, so that *lenient* may be /'liːniːənt/, /'liːnɪənt/, or /'liːnjənt/. There are other cases, though, where only /j/ is possible, as in *failure* /'feɪljə/ (which can only be pronounced as two syllables; compare *dahlia*, which in RP may either rhyme with it as a disyllable, or alternatively be pronounced trisyllabically as /'deɪliːə ~ 'deɪlɪə/). In words where some speakers have syllable-final /ns/, such as *fence* /fens/, others have /nts/, thus /fents/; and where the majority have /ntʃ/, as in *lunch* /lʌntʃ/, some have /nʃ/, thus /lʌnʃ/. (*EPD* writes these omissible sounds in italics.) Some people switch between variant pronunciations such as these in line with extraneous factors such as tempo and formality.

Two further cases of variation are particularly worthy of the EFL learner's attention: stress shifting and weak forms. Stress shifting affects those words which have more than one stress in their basic form: ˌun'known, asˌsoci'ation, ˌthir'teen, ˌcircum'stantial. I have followed the usual convention of marking the first stress with the lowered mark, as a "secondary stress", on the grounds that this syllable normally never bears the intonation nucleus: but the important point is that where the following word bears an accent then double-stressed words of the kind we are considering shift their strong stress onto the first element: *an 'unknown 'author, as'sociation ' football, 'thirteen 'people, 'circumstantial 'evidence*. Weak forms are the special connected-speech variants characterizing most of the commoner form words (words of the minor syntactic classes). In citation, in isolation, and when accented, *at, from, can, are* /æt, frɒm, kæn, ɑː(r)/; otherwise they are /ət, frəm, kən, ə(r)/. (Note also the "syntactic gap rule" whereby a strong form is obligatory, even though unaccented, in cases such as *he was shot at by a gunman, that's where he comes from, you do it better than I can, his are nicer than mine are*.)

It seems to me to be highly desirable for dictionaries to draw explicit attention to these last two types of variation between the pronunciation of a word in isolation and its likely pronunciation in connected speech. LDOCE 1978 introduces a special wedge symbol to remind the user of possible stress shift (thus /ˌʌn'nəʊn ◄/); *EPD* is wordier (". . . *also* 'ʌnn-, ʌn'n-, *according to sentence stress*"). Many dictionaries totally ignore the phenomenon. Weak forms are included in the relevant pronunciation entries of the phonetically more enlightened dictionaries, but ignored in many others (including some large bilingual dictionaries). [Cf. Stein, this volume, pp. 42–43—ed.]

3. Choice of notation system

The basic decision an English lexicographer must make is whether to apply a transcription system based on "respelling", or one making use of proper phonetic symbols. Various hybrid systems are also possible.

In monolingual English dictionaries aimed at the native-speaker market respelling systems are still very widely used. In this type of system the pronunciation of *weak* is shown either as "week" or as "wēk", while *brooch* appears as "broach" or "brōch" and *father* as "fah′dher", "fä′dhər" or the like. It is not possible to design a respelling system for English that avoids both diacritics and arbitrary conventions: the diphthong in *price* and the distinction between *look* and *Luke* necessitate one or other of them (either "prīs", etc., or a special convention such as "prys"; either "lo͝ok, lo͞ok" or a special convention such as "look, loohk"). There are also difficulties with words such as *real*, with no satisfactory respelling to show the pronunciation written in *EPD* as /rɪəl/ and no way to make clear that *Korea* and *career* are usually homophones in RP. Nevertheless, respelling systems can with care be designed so as to convey extensive polylectal information to the reader who is patient enough to explore the notation conventions carefully, as in the recent GID, mentioned above.

Anyone seriously interested in pronunciation has to get to grips with phonetic transcription. The use of IPA symbols in English monolingual dictionaries for the native speaker is gaining ground in Britain (though not in America), and in the EFL world the use of phonetic symbols has long been accepted as essential. Wherever the pronunciation model adopted is British, the symbols used are those of the International Phonetic Association, based on the works of Daniel Jones. There is, however, no unique IPA way of representing the sounds of a language, and for English in particular there are several slightly different competing systems—a situation much deprecated by publishers, learners, and authors. Three representative systems are set out in Table 1. The first, referred to here as "Jones", is the one used by Jones in his *Outline* (1975) and editions 1–12 of *EPD*. This form of transcription is characterized especially by the use of the length mark (":") as the sole differentiation between the vowels of *feet* and *fit*, *Luke* and *look* (/fiːt, fit, luːk, luk/). This is convenient in that it reduced the number of special symbols needed, but rather seriously misleading from the point of view of the foreign

Table 1.

1. (Jones)	2. (Windsor Lewis)	3. (Gimson)	Exemplificatory keywords
iː	i	iː	*bead, fleece, knee*
i	ɪ	ɪ	*bid, kit*
e	e	e	*bed, dress*
æ	æ	æ	*bad, trap*
ɑː	ɑ	ɑː	*bard, bath, start, palm*
ɔ	o	ɒ	*cod, lot, cloth*
ɔː	ɔ	ɔː	*board, north, force, thought*
u	ʊ	ʊ	*could, foot*
uː	u	uː	*mood, goose, two*
ʌ	ʌ	ʌ	*bud, strut, love*
əː	ɜ	ɜː	*bird, nurse, fur*
ə	ə	ə	*letter, comma*
ei	eɪ	eɪ	*made, face, hay*
ou	əʊ	əʊ	*mode, goat, know*
ai	ɑɪ	ʌɪ	*bide, price, high*
au	ɑʊ	aʊ	*loud, mouth, how*
ɔi	ɔɪ	ɔɪ	*Boyd, choice, joy*
iə	ɪə	ɪə	*beard, near, idea*
ɛə	eə	eə	*bared, square*
uə	ʊə	ʊə	*moored, cure*

learner, who needs to be aware that these vowel distinctions rest primarily on quality (timbre) rather than on quantity (length). Indeed, in a word such as *teacher*, where the "long" first vowel is subject to the clipping effects both of the following voiceless consonant /tʃ/ and of the following unstressed vowel, its actual phonetic length is pretty short. If hearsay is to be believed, Jones himself was dissatisfied in later life with this transcription, and retained it only on the insistence of his publishers (and indeed used other transcriptions in other works on English).

The second, "Windsor Lewis" (e.g. 1972), is chosen as representative of "qualitative" transcription systems, where length marks are abandoned and the *feet–fit, Luke–look* distinctions are shown only by special letter shapes (/fit, fɪt, luk, lʊk/; some writers, notably Abercrombie and Ladefoged, use "ɷ" rather than "ʊ"). Although this type of transcription seems particularly suitable for teaching phonetics to native speakers of English, who do not need to be reminded of underlying (inherent) length differences, it is open to the objection that it is easily misread, since the rather similar letter shapes used for the long-short pairs can readily be confused by the bleary eye. It has certainly not proved a success in the EFL publishing world, where the third transcription presented in the table is now gradually consolidating its victory.

This one, "Gimson", is that used by the current, fourteenth, edition of *EPD*, edited by Gimson, and differs only trivially from that used in Gimson 1962 [Cf. Kirkpatrick, this volume, p. 9—ed.). (It is a characteristic straw in the wind that O'Connor's popular manual *Better English Pronunciation* has gone over from the "Jones" transcription in the first edition to the "Gimson" one in the current, second, edition.) The Gimson notation gets the best of both worlds, at the expense of some redundancy: *feet* /fiːt/ and *Luke* /luːk/ are distinguished from *fit* /fɪt/ and *look* /lʊk/ both by the use of distinctive letter shapes and by the presence vs. absence of length marks. This enhances their visual distinctiveness while reminding the foreign learner that he must make quality differences, too, between the paired long and short vowels.

Consonants are shown uniformly in all IPA transcriptions of English, with /θ, ð/ for the voiceless and voiced dental fricatives respectively (*think*, *this*), /ʃ, ʒ/ for the palato-alveolar fricatives (*mission*, *vision*), /tʃ, dʒ/ for the palato-alveolar affricates (*church*, *judge*), and /ŋ/ for the velar nasal (*singing*). This helps resolve the ambiguity in orthographic *g* and *ng*, which remains a potential problem in respelling systems (thus *give* /gɪv/, *gin* /dʒɪn/; *finger* /'fɪŋgə/, *singer* /'sɪŋə/, *ginger* /'dʒɪndʒə/). The IPA-recommended way of showing stress is by a vertical mark before the syllable concerned, thus *above* /ə'bʌv/. Until the 1920's, however, the IPA used to recommend an acute accent, thus /ə′bʌv/; and such is the cultural lag in lexicography that there are still dictionaries on sale (e.g. Collin 1982) which use an acute accent and claim it as IPA approved; the acute accent is also used with IPA symbols in Collin 1981. Other conventions found include an accent mark above the letter, thus /əbʌ́v/ and, in respelling systems, a mark following the stressed syllable, thus abŭv′.

The advice I would give to the compiler of a bilingual dictionary who comes in search of a simple rule for acceptable English pronunciation entries is to follow the current edition of *EPD*, selecting the first alternative offered in the case of words where several are given.

References

Collin, P. H. *et al.*, *Harrap's Shorter French and English Dictionary*. Harrap, 1982.

Collin, P. H., *Harrap's 2000 Word English Dictionary*. Harrap, 1981.

Delbridge, A. (ed.), *The Macquarie Dictionary*. Macquarie Library, 1981.

Gimson, A.C., *An Introduction to the Pronunciation of English*. Edward Arnold, 1962, 1970, 1980.

Hanks, P. (ed.), *Collins English Dictionary*. Collins, 1979.

Ilson, R. (ed.), *Reader's Digest Great Illustrated Dictionary*. Reader's Digest, 1984.

Jones, D., *An Outline of English Phonetics*. Cambridge University Press, 1975 (previous editions, Heffer).

Jones, D., *English Pronouncing Dictionary*. Dent, 1977. Fourteenth edition, revised by A. C. Gimson.

Kenyon, J. S. and Knott, T. A., *A Pronouncing Dictionary of American English*. Merriam, 1953.

Kirkpatrick, E. M. (ed.), *Chambers Twentieth Century Dictionary*. Chambers, 1983.

Martinet, A. and Walter, H., *Dictionnaire de la prononciation française dans son usage réel*. France-Expansion, 1973.

Nihalani, P., Tongue, R. K. and Hosali, P., *Indian and British English. A Handbook of Usage and Pronunciation*. Oxford University Press, Delhi, 1979.

O'Connor, J. D., *Better English Pronunciation*. Cambridge University Press, 1980.

Procter, P. (ed.), *Longman Dictionary of Contemporary English*. Longman, 1978.

Trim, J. L. M. "English Standard Pronunciation", *English Language Teaching* **16.1**:28–37, 1961.

Wells, J. C., *Accents of English*. Cambridge University Press, 1982.

Windsor Lewis, J., *A Concise Pronouncing Dictionary of British and American English*. Oxford University Press, 1972.

GRAMMAR IN THE DICTIONARY

HOWARD JACKSON

City of Birmingham Polytechnic

If you look a word up in a dictionary—any dictionary—a number of different kinds of information will be presented to you. Some of that information will be grammatical. In this paper, we are going to investigate the nature of the grammatical information found in dictionaries and evaluate its usefulness for the second-language user of English monolingual dictionaries.

Grammar vs Dictionary

Arguably, Grammar and Dictionary are complementary parts of the overall description of a language. This applies whether the aim of the description is the general linguistic one of providing a comprehensive account of a language, or whether the aim is an applied one of serving the needs of an identifiable group of language users. It could be maintained, however, that language users have recourse more to the Dictionary than to the Grammar, whether they are first-language users or second-language users. Indeed, it has been argued (Al-Kasimi, 1977:50) that a Dictionary should "provide the foreign learner with all the information he needs without referring him to handbooks of grammar". Nevertheless, a Dictionary depends on a grammatical description, either explicitly or implicitly, since all Dictionaries use grammatical terms (e.g. "noun", "verb intransitive") which have their characterization in the Grammar. Similarly, a Grammar presupposes a Dictionary, since in the Grammar lexical items are treated by and large only in terms of class-membership, not as individual lexical counters—despite the attention devoted in Grammars to certain individual "function words" (e.g. *if, should, the*).

Rarely are the links between Dictionary and Grammar made explicit in lexicographical practice: the notable exception is the *Grammar of Contemporary English* (Quirk *et al.*, 1972) and the *Longman Dictionary of Contemporary English* (1978), written as a complementary pair. Perhaps also an exception is the *Oxford Advanced Learner's Dictionary of Current English* (1981) which presupposes Hornby's work on grammar (especially the verb patterns), the essentials of which are included in the front-matter of that dictionary.

Let us understand what we mean by "Grammar" and "Dictionary". A Grammar is concerned with the general rules affecting the classes of items in a language. A Dictionary is concerned with the operation of individual lexical items. That is to put the distinction at its crudest. More precisely, a Grammar describes the syntactic arrangements of classes of items; it describes the kinds of grammatical "meanings" (e.g. plurality, tense) that may be realized in a language, and the formal means (e.g. inflectional endings) by which those meanings are realized. A Dictionary aims to list the lexical items (words, idioms, other fixed expressions) in a language and to give a description of their meaning and usage; within "usage" will be included the part a lexical item plays in the grammatical system of a language.

Grammar in the Dictionary

Following on from what we have said, there are four kinds of grammatical information that we might expect to find in dictionary entries [Cf. Whitcut, this volume, pp. 75–76—ed]. Firstly, there is information about the inflections that a lexical item might have, particularly when these are not deducible from the general statements of the Grammar. Secondly, each item in the Dictionary is traditionally provided with a "part-of-speech" or "word-class" label, e.g. "noun", "preposition". As we shall see, this label is primarily of a syntactic nature, giving information on the operation of an item in the grammatical system of the language. Thirdly, a dictionary entry may be provided with information of a more explicitly syntactic nature; for example, verbs are traditionally marked as "transitive" or "intransitive". For the second-language user of a Dictionary, this information may be of particular importance. Fourthly, grammatical—especially syntactic—information may be provided implicitly or covertly by means of the illustrative examples that may form part of a dictionary entry.

We will now consider in turn each of these kinds of grammatical information that may be found in dictionary entries, what contribution they make in the context of the Dictionary, and how they may be presented.

Inflections

Inflectional affixes—in English only suffixes—realize grammatical meanings or functions, e.g. "plural number" in the noun, "past tense" in the verb. Usually they have a form which is either constant, e.g. the "present participle" suffix (-ing), or at least predictable phonologically and orthographically, e.g. the 3rd person singular present tense suffix. Such "regular" inflections are described in the Grammar and do not need to be repeated for each relevant item in the Dictionary. However, where the form of an inflection for a particular lexical item does not follow the general pattern, i.e. is "irregular", then this does need to be indicated in the Dictionary; it is not predictable from the general rules of the Grammar. Such is the case, for example, with the plural of the noun *tooth* (*teeth* /ti:θ/), or the past tense of the verb *keep* (*kept* /kept/). This is the practice followed by the *Longman Dictionary of Contemporary English* (LDOCE) and the *Oxford Advanced Learner's Dictionary of Current English* (ALD).

An interesting case is presented in English by the comparative and superlative forms of adjectives, where there is only a small number of irregular forms (*bad—worse—worst*, etc.), but where there is an alternation between an inflectional suffix (-er, -est) and the use of *more/most* before the adjective.

Shorter adjectives (one syllable) usually take the inflectional suffix, while longer ones (three syllables or more) usually take *more/most*; but there are some adjectives (mostly of two syllables—e.g. *handsome*—or compound—e.g. *large-hearted*) where both forms of the comparative and superlative are possible. In the *ALD*, all adjectives that take only the inflectional suffix are marked as such, while those that can take *more/most* are not marked. In the *LDOCE*, those taking *more/most* remain unmarked, while a differentiation is made (by means of codes that refer to an interpretative table elsewhere in the dictionary) between adjectives that are only ever suffixed and those that may form comparative and superlative in either way. Clearly, a learner needs maximally differentiated information in order to perform correctly and to be aware of available choices in the language.

Parts of Speech

If a Dictionary gives no other information of a grammatical nature, it is expected to indicate which part-of-speech or word-class a lexical item belongs to, i.e. whether it is classed as a noun or a verb or an adjective, etc. But we may well question the validity of this hallowed practice of lexicographical tradition. What kind of information are we being given when we are told that a lexical item is a "noun" or a "preposition"? And why is it important for a dictionary user to know the word-class to which an item belongs?

Firstly, the word-class label is an instruction about the kinds of inflections that are appropriate to the lexical item. The label "noun" implies the possibility of a "plural" and a "possessive" inflection, though it should be noted that not all nouns do inflect in these ways in actual usage (e.g. *wisdom* does not inflect for "plural", and a "possessive" inflection is highly unlikely with *lack*)—a grammatical fact that is also of relevance to the dictionary user.

Secondly, and perhaps more importantly, the word-class label provides basic information about the syntactic operation of a lexical item. To be told that an item is a "noun" is to be informed about the places at which it may occur in syntactic structure, i.e. as head of a nominal phrase ("five lively Spanish *dances*"). Similarly, an "adjective" is an item that may occur either as a modifier before the noun in a nominal phrase ("a *good* book") or as head of an adjectival phrase in the predicate of a clause ("our visit was very *rewarding*").

The part-of-speech label in dictionary entries is questionable not because it provides information irrelevant to the dictionary user, but because it does not provide sufficient information of a grammatical (inflectional and especially syntactic) kind. We have noted already that not all nouns are found with a "plural" or a "possessive" inflection. Similarly, not all adjectives may occur as modifier in a nominal phrase; nor may all occur as head of an adjectival phrase in predicative position. We will take up this point again (in the next section) when we consider the marking of syntactic operation.

Before we do that, let us consider two further points about part-of-speech labels. Firstly, let us reiterate the point made earlier that grammatical terms like "noun" and "preposition" depend on a prior Grammar for their characterization. For most Dictionaries this Grammar is implicit, the generally understood and accepted linguistic knowledge of the educated person; consequently, the part-of-speech labels used are the traditional eight—noun, verb, adjective, adverb, pronoun, conjunction, preposition, interjection. The *ALD* operates essentially with this system. The *LDOCE*, depending on the *Grammar of Contemporary English*, also introduces the term "determiner", for items such as *this*, *the* (marked in *ALD* as "def art"), and the modifying use of *several*.

Secondly, it should be noted that many lexical items belong to more than one word-class; e.g. *outside* may be a noun, an adjective, an adverb or a preposition; *many* may be a determiner or a pronoun. Often, this difference in word-class membership (i.e. in syntactic function) is taken as the basis on which to make a lexical differentiation either into separate senses or into separate headwords.

Syntactic Operation

Part of the information that a dictionary user—rightly—expects to gain from a dictionary entry for a lexical item is how to use that item in his own language performance. Included within this information on use must be a specification of the syntactic operation of the lexical item, how it fits as an individual item into the general syntactic patterns of the language. The Dictionary must give this information, since, while the user can be expected to come to the Dictionary with a knowledge of the general rules of Grammar, the place of an individual lexical item within those rules (e.g. which of them apply to that item) is part of the idiosyncratic information about the item.

Arguably, this information is particularly crucial in the case of verbs, especially if one regards the verb as the element which determines to a large extent which other elements may be present in its clause. This is the assumption underlying Hornby's "verb patterns" (Hornby 1954, 1975), which form the basis of the syntactic specification of the verbs in the *ALD*. It is also the assumption behind the description of verb "complementation" in the *Grammar of Contemporary English* (Ch 12), which informs the syntactic specification of verbs in the *LDOCE*.

Both these dictionaries recognize, then, that the traditional specification of verbs as "transitive" or "intransitive" provides insufficient information to enable the learner to build acceptable clauses. The dictionary entry needs to specify in detail which clause patterns a verb may enter, what complementation a verb may take, which items are obligatory or optional or deletable. Additionally, the dictionary entry needs to specify whether a verb cannot undergo a particular rule of the Grammar, e.g. if it is unable to form "progressive" tenses or to enter the "passive" construction.

Consider, for example, the verb *imagine*. With this verb one can build clauses such as the following: "You can imagine how they must have felt" (subject—verb—object: *wh*-clause); "I can't imagine not having a job" (subject—verb—object: *-ing*-clause). "Can you imagine the choir singing in the Albert Hall?" (subject—verb—object: NP + *-ing*-clause); "You must imagine that the whole world is at peace" (subject—verb—object: *that*-clause).

Generalizing, we can say that *imagine* is basically a monotransitive verb (its complementation includes just one object), but that the object may be realized by a variety of elements: nominal phrase, finite clause (*that*-clause, *wh*-clause), non-finite clause (*-ing*-clause) both with and without preceding nominal phrase. These idiosyncratic syntactic facts about *imagine* need to be noted in its dictionary entry, along with the fact that *imagine* does not usually enter "progressive" tenses—except in expressions like "You're *imagining/seeing/hearing* things (that don't really exist)!" One might also note the frequent use of the modal verb *can* with *imagine*, which comes out in the examples above; but here we are perhaps approaching a fineness of detail that is impractical and perhaps unnecessary: the lexicographer must decide. The reader is invited to examine the entries for *imagine* in the *ALD* and the *LDOCE* to judge how well these dictionaries specify the syntactic operation of this verb.

What is true for the specification of the syntactic operation of verbs is also true, to a lesser extent, for members of other word classes. Nouns, for example, besides not being universally marked for "plural" and "possessive", also vary in the kinds of determiners that may precede them in nominal phrases. This variation correlates with the distinction between "countable" nouns and "uncountable" (or "mass") nouns. The indefinite article, for example, cannot usually be used with mass nouns (* "a wisdom"), nor can quantifiers like *many* and *several*. Some nouns may be used both as countables and as mass nouns. While all nouns may be post-modified by relative clauses (a general rule of grammar that does not need rehearsing in the Dictionary), only some nouns may be postmodified by an appositive *that*-clause (e.g. "the decision *that payment should be suspended*" by contrast with "the decision that |which| ø we discussed").

In respect of adjectives, we have noted that some are restricted in position of occurrence to their "attributive" position (as modifier in a nominal phrase) or to "predicative" position (as head of an adjectival phrase in the clause predicate). Some adjectives and nouns may be followed by a "complement", which may take the form of a prepositional phrase ("afraid/fear *of the dark*"), or an infinitive clause ("determined/determination *to get his own way*"), or a *that*-clause ("sorry/sorrow *that you cannot come to the party*").

Most adverbs function as head of adverb phrases, though here a distinction may be made between the adjunct, conjunct and disjunct functions of adverbs (cf. Quirk *et al.*, 1972: 268; Jackson, 1982: 79–80). Some adverbs function only as modifiers in adjectival and adverb phrases (e.g. *extremely*, *very*, *quite*), and some may function both as modifier and as head (e.g. *highly*, *enormously*).

All these facts about the syntactic operation of certain members of certain word classes are particular facts about individual lexical items, and are not deducible from the general rules of grammar (unless the Grammar is going to contain comprehensive lists of which lexical items undergo which rules of the Grammar). They are appropriately stated in the dictionary entries for the lexical items. One might, however, argue whether they should be stated explicitly in some way, or implicitly.

Implicit Grammar

In the *LDOCE* entry for *enormously*, the syntactic designation is just "adv"; but the entry contains the following illustrative examples: "enormously rich/it interests me enormously". The fact that *enormously* may function syntactically either as a modifier or as a head is not stated explicitly, but implicitly through the illustrative examples. It might be argued that a syntactic distinction of this kind is relatively minor and thus more appropriately indicated by means of example than by an explicit designation.

Cowie (1978: 129), discussing the role of illustrative examples in the *ALD*, argues that they have three functions: "indicate the syntactic distribution of words in their various senses"; "throw light on the meaning of the words"; "encourage the learner to compose sentences which are lexically, as well as syntactically, new" (cf. Al-Kasimi, 1977: 90–91). Al-Kasimi maintains that illustrative examples should not take the place of grammatical or semantic statements, but, as we have seen with the *enormously* example from *LDOCE*, there may be a case for the examples to convey an implicit grammatical statement in some instances.

Certainly it is the case that illustrative examples perform a useful backup to the explicit grammatical designation, in clarifying in real language data what is stated abstractly and generally. It is in the illustrative examples also that the convergence between grammar, meaning and usage takes place: carefully chosen examples can illustrate what is typical of the lexical and grammatical usage of a lexical item. They, thus, have an important function in the overall grammatical statement in the Dictionary.

Conclusion

In the foregoing we have investigated the kinds of grammatical information that need to be included in a Dictionary, if the Dictionary is to "give for each item all pertinent grammatical identification" (Gleason, 1967: 102). Two further points remain to be discussed: the first concerns the presentation of the grammatical information; the second concerns the importance of the grammatical information for the foreign learner.

How should grammatical information be presented in the Dictionary? Because of the restriction of space that dictionaries always suffer under, it is unavoidable that some form of coding needs to be used; e.g. the *ALD* for each verb indicates which "verb pattern" is appropriate by a series of numbers that refer the user to a comprehensive list with examples in the front-matter of the dictionary (cf. *imagine* VP6A,C,9,10,16B,19A,C,25). Unfortunately, it seems to be the case that the more detailed the grammatical information, the more elaborate must the coding system become: a comparison of *ALD* and *LDOCE* in this respect is instructive. The lexicographer must then begin to balance understandability and ease of use with comprehensiveness and overall usefulness of the Dictionary. Perhaps this is where the subtle interplay between grammatical statement and illustrative example could come into its own.

But how important to the foreign learner is the grammatical information in a

Dictionary? It might be argued that a learner is informed of the grammatical usage of individual lexical items when he learns particular rules and patterns in his language course, or when he sees items in use in reading passages and the like. But, on the other hand, inclusion of grammatical information in the Dictionary implies that the learner is going to use the Dictionary in order to foster his productive use of language, rather than just as an aid to comprehension. That, indeed, is the point: the inclusion of grammatical information in the Dictionary is a contribution to making the language learner an independent learner, to enabling the learner to produce for himself correct and appropriate sentences in the language he is learning.

References

Al-Kasimi, Ali, M., *Linquistics and Bilingual Dictionaries*. E. J. Brill, 1977.

Cowie, A. P., "The place of illustrative material and collocations in the design of a learner's dictionary", *In Honour of A. S. Hornby*. OUP, 1978.

Gleason, H. A., "The Relation of Lexicon and Grammar" in *Problems in Lexicography*, Indiana University, 1967.

Hornby, A. S., *A Guide to Patterns and Usage in English*, OUP, 1954. (2nd edition 1975).

Hornby, A. S. (ed)., *Oxford Advanced Learner's Dictionary of Current English*. OUP, 3rd edition 1981.

Jackson, H., *Analyzing English*. Pergamon, 2nd edition 1982.

Longman Dictionary of Contemporary English. Longman, 1978.

Quirk, R., Greenbaum, S., Leech, G., Svartvik, J., *A Grammar of Contemporary English*. Longman, 1972.

COLLOCATIONS AND IDIOMS

MORTON BENSON
University of Pennsylvania

Introduction

This paper treats collocations and idioms in dictionaries of English. Such constructions are of special interest to dictionary users who are learning English as a second or foreign language. These remarks refer to both monolingual dictionaries of English and to bilingual dictionaries that have English as their source language.[1]*

Collocations

By *collocation* we mean a group of words that occurs repeatedly, i.e. recurs, in a language. These "recurrent phrases" can be divided into *grammatical collocations* and *lexical collocations*.

Grammatical Collocations

In his *Aspects of the Theory of Syntax* (p. 191) Noam Chomsky points out that *decide on a boat*, meaning "choose (to buy) a boat", is a *close construction*, whereas *decide on a boat*, meaning "make a decision while on a boat", is a *loose association*. In this paper we will use the term *grammatical collocation* for "close construction" and *free construction* or *free combination* for "loose association". Any native speaker of English feels that *decide on* "choose" represents a unit; the two words "collocate" with each other. On the other hand, *decide on* "decide while on" is a free construction, consisting of a verb followed by an adverbial prepositional phrase. It is obvious that dictionaries should include collocations rather than free constructions. We will attempt now to define *grammatical collocation*: a grammatical collocation is a recurrent combination, usually consisting of a dominant word (verb, noun, adjective), followed by a "grammatical" word, typically a preposition. Examples of verb + preposition collocations are: *abide by, abstain from, account for, accuse (somebody) of, adhere to, agonize over, aim at, alert (somebody) to, allow for, answer for (to), approve of, atone for, avail (oneself) of*, etc. Examples of noun + preposition collocations are: *abstinence from, access to, accusation against, acquiescence in (to), admiration for, advantage over, allegiance to, amazement at, ambassador to, analogy between (to, with), anathema to, anger at (towards), antidote against (for, to), apathy towards*, etc. Examples of adjective + preposition collocations are: *absent from, accountable to,*

* Superscript numbers are to Notes at end of article.

61

acquainted with, adept at (in), adequate for (to), adjacent to, afraid of, aghast at, alert to, alien to, allied to (with), aloof from, amazed at, angry about (at, with), answerable for (to), etc.

Note that the collocations above are *not* "idioms": their meanings are more or less inferrable from the meanings of their parts, even though the prepositions in the collocations are not predictable.

Dictionaries should provide such collocations at the entry for the dominant word (verb, noun, or adjective). The leading British learner's dictionaries—the *Longman Dictionary of Contemporary English* (LDOCE) and A. S. Hornby, *Oxford Advanced Learner's Dictionary of Current English* (ALD)—do give a large number of grammatical collocations. American general-use dictionaries are, on the other hand, unsatisfactory; they do not give a sufficient number of grammatical collocations.

Lexical Collocations

Lexical collocations, in contrast to grammatical collocations, contain no subordinate element; they usually consist of two "equal" lexical components. The major types of lexical collocations are: adjective + noun combinations, noun + verb combinations, and verb + noun combinations. Heretofore, the treatment of lexical collocations in dictionaries of English has been unsatisfactory. We can expect, however, that the situation will be improved.

Apresyan, Mel'čuk, and Žolkovsky, working originally in the Soviet Union, have made a significant contribution to the treatment of collocations.[2] They proposed a new type of dictionary called the *Explanatory and Combinatory Dictionary* (ECD). The ECD method is to subject a relatively small number of carefully selected entries (approximately two thousand) to a very detailed grammatical and lexical treatment. Each entry is arranged in exactly the same way and provides exactly the same type of information. The entry contains the definition, pertinent morphological and syntactic information, lexical functions, phraseology, and a discussion of synonyms and near synonyms.

The most significant innovation of the ECD is the concept of *lexical functions*. Over forty functions have been identified. They are designated by Latin- or Greek-sounding names. To be sure, some of the functions are not new; they have been utilized in dictionaries for many decades. For example, the first function named is *Syn* (synonym), i.e. in all ECD entries, synonyms of the headwords are given.

Some of the ECD lexical functions seem overly intricate or rare, and would not be suited for inclusion in a general-use dictionary. For example, the function *Figur* (figurative) somehow produces, in the entry for *night*, the collocation *cover of night*. A major drawback of the ECD approach, from the viewpoint of the lexicographer who compiles general-use dictionaries, is that some lexical functions produce *free combinations*. An example is the function *Caus* (cause), which expresses the meaning of "to cause", "to bring about". However, the verb *to cause*, and some of its synonyms, combine freely with hundreds of nouns (which often have a negative meaning). These combinations are predictable. Let us cite a few examples showing nouns beginning with the letter *d*: *to cause—damage, danger, deafness, a death, a debacle, decay, decompression, defeat, a defect, a deficiency, deflation, a deformity, degeneracy, dehydration*, etc. A general-use dictionary would be needlessly swamped by the inclusion of all such combinations.

Many other verb and noun combinations that would be required by ECD functions also represent free combinations: *build bridges (houses, roads), cook meat (potatoes, vegetables), grow apples (bananas, corn), make* or *manufacture blackboards (cars, shelves), prepare breakfast (dinner, lunch)*, etc.

On the other hand, some of the ECD functions do suggest significant innovations for lexicography. They are of considerable importance to compilers of general-use dictionaries. An example is *Magn* (magnus) meaning 'of the highest degree'. We will cite several examples of this function as applied to English nouns beginning with the letter *a*: *reckless abandon, a confirmed addict, outright (naked) aggression, mortal agony, a chronic alcoholic, a rank amateur, a burning ambition, deep animosity, outstanding aptitude, an irrefutable argument, a vile atrocity, an all-out (full-scale) attack*, etc. However, it is not feasible or desirable to include all such possible collocations in a dictionary. No general-purpose dictionary can be expected, for example, to give all the collocations produced by *Magn* for the noun *crime*: *an abominable, atrocious, contemptible, deplorable, despicable, disgusting, fiendish, foul, heinous, hideous, horrible, monstrous, outrageous, repugnant, shameful, vile* (etc.)—*crime*.

Another important ECD function is *Func* (function), meaning the "basic action" performed by a noun. Here are several examples of collocations with nouns that begin with the letters *a* and *b*: *adjectives modify, airplanes fly, alarms go off (sound), bees buzz (sting, swarm), bells ring, birds chirp (fly, sing), blizzards rage, blood circulates (flows)*, etc. It must be added that a rigid and undiscriminating application of the ECD function *Func* in a general-use dictionary would be unwarranted. It would require the inclusion of such predictable and unnecessary combinations as *bakers bake, boxers box, cooks cook, dancers dance, fencers fence, fighters fight*, etc.

We have just seen that several of the ECD functions are of vital interest to the compiler of a general-purpose dictionary. These functions must be utilized, however, with considerable restraint, caution, and common sense if the inclusion of unneeded free combinations is to be avoided.

We propose that the following types of lexical collocations be included in general-use dictionaries of English. Some of these collocational types are suggested by the ECD; others are not. All of the collocations should be given at the *noun* entry.

1. Noun+verb

We have in mind here the unpredictable collocations suggested by the ECD function *Func*: *adjectives modify, bells ring*, etc. Additional examples were given above.

2. Adjective+noun

Some of these collocations are suggested by the ECD function *Magn*: *a confirmed bachelor*, *a pitched battle*, *pure chance*, *a responsive chord*, *well-informed circles*, *keen competition*, *grave concern*, *sincere condolences*, etc.

3. Verb+noun CA collocations

These collocations consist of a verb denoting *creation* and/or *activation* and a noun. Here are examples of collocations with verbs denoting *creation*: *compile a dictionary*, *make an impression*, *draw up a list*, *compose music*, *set a record*, *reach a verdict*, *inflict a wound*. Other verbs in CA collocations express the concept of *activation*: *set an alarm*, *roll a hoop*, *fly a kite*, *launch a missile*, *punch a time clock*, *spin a top*, *wind a watch*.[3]

In some instances, the same noun collocates with one verb (or verbs) to denote creation and with another verb (or verbs) to denote activation: *establish a principle* (=creation)—*apply a principle* (=activation); *draw up a will* (=creation)—*execute a will* (=activation); *pronounce (pass) a sentence* (=creation)—*carry out (execute) a sentence* (=activation).

In many instances the meanings *creation* and *activation* are united in one verb: *call an alert*, *display bravery*, *hatch a conspiracy*, *award custody*, *impose an embargo*, *produce friction*, *inflict an injustice*, *commit murder*, *perform an operation*, *offer opposition*, *pose a question*, *lay a smoke screen*, etc.

CA collocations are arbitrary and non-predictable. Non-native speakers cannot cope with them; they must have a guide. They have no way of knowing that one says in English *make an estimate* (but not **make an estimation*), *commit treason* (but not **commit treachery*). In English one says *commit fraud* and *perpetrate fraud*. However, only the collocation *commit suicide* is possible; one does not say **perpetrate suicide*. One says *bake a cake*, but *make pancakes*. The expression *do graduate work* is used frequently, but one does not say **do graduate studies*. (One does say: *pursue graduate studies*.) One *delivers* or *administers a rebuke*, but not a *reproach*. (The latter noun, like many others, apparently enters into no CA collocations.) One *makes a mistake*, but not a *misprint*. One can say *hold a funeral*, but not **hold a burial*.

The arbitrary nature of CA collocations is demonstrated forcefully when they are translated into foreign languages. The verb in each language is often "different". For example, the English collocation *to give a lecture* is rendered in French as *faire une conférence*, in German as *einen Vortrag halten*, and in Russian as *pročitat' lekciju*. Many other collocational differences could be cited. These contrasts bear witness to far-reaching implications for the teaching of English as a second/foreign language and for foreign-language teaching in general.

Even the native speaker may need at times to refer to a list of CA collocations. Many may not know which verbs collocate with such nouns as the following: *acquittal, acumen, acupuncture, afterburners, attitude, authority, barrage, bayonet, bench warrant, blood test, Caesarean section, cartwheel, charm, circuit breaker, cloture, copyright, council, counsel, coup de grâce, coup d'état*, etc. A native speaker of AE (American English), who says *to take up a collection*, will not know which verb collocates with a colloquial BE (British English) synonym of a *collection*, namely a *whip-round* (*have*). Speakers of BE prefer *to have a bath*, *have a walk*; AE speakers invariably *take a bath*, *take a walk*. CE (Common or World English) speakers *make a decision*; BE speakers can also *take a decision*. Most speakers of AE will not know which verb collocates with the BE a *moonlight flit* (*do*).

CA collocations for polysemous nouns are extremely important. For example, the entry for the noun *line* should have the following collocations: *draw a line* (on paper); *form a line* (= line up); *drop smb. a line*. The entry for *operation* should have: *perform an operation* (in a hospital); *carry out (conduct) an operation* (on the battlefield). The entry for *sentence* should have: *pronounce (pass) sentence* (in court); *form (formulate, compose) a sentence* (in a grammar class), etc.

Thus, we have seen that CA collocations represent a basic, vital element of lexical combinability. *They are essential to the generation of acceptable English sentences and should become an obligatory element in dictionaries of English.* It must be emphasized that CA collocations are to be included in *noun* entries. This arrangement allows the user of the dictionary to find collocations that existing dictionaries, thesauruses, or handbooks do not provide. No presently available source shows which verbs collocate with which nouns. The inclusion of CA collocations at verb entries would not help most seekers of collocations who want to find out which verb is used with a certain noun. The usual question is: which verb collocates with *plea*? Or: What does one do to a *plea*? The answer, of course, is *enter (make) a plea*.

As pointed out above in our discussion of the ECD, free combinations can be generated when verbs and nouns are paired. Predictable free combinations should *not* be entered in a general-purpose dictionary even if, strictly speaking, they convey the meanings of "creation" or "activation". Thus, the lexicographer need not include combinations such as *build a bridge*, *cause damage*, *grow apples*, *make shelves*. (For additional examples, see above.) On the other hand, the lexicographer should never hesitate to include important unpredictable verb + noun collocations even if they do not mean "creation" or "activation". Examples are: *do the laundry*, *decline a noun*, *take one's seat*, *carry a story*, *confirm a suspicion*, *resist temptation*, *renew a visa*, etc.

4. Verb + noun EN collocations

These collocations consist of a verb denoting *eradication* and/or *nullification* and a noun.[4] Typical examples are the following: *reject an appeal*, *recall a bid*, *lift a blockade*, *invalidate a clause*, *break a code*, *eliminate a competitor* (from a contest), *abrogate a constitution*, *reverse a decision*, *negate (nullify) the effects* (of something), *dispel fear*, *squander a fortune*, *destroy a friendship*, *demolish (raze, tear down) a house*, *repeal a law*, *revoke a license*, *annul a marriage*, *suspend martial law*, *scrub (cancel) a mission*, etc. The examples demonstrate that EN collocations are indispensable for the generation of acceptable English sentences.

As with CA collocations, lexicographers should not enter in their dictionaries predictable free EN combinations. For example, the verb *to destroy* can be used with a very large number of nouns denoting physical objects; these should not be entered. Examples are: *to destroy—a barn, bridge, building, city, document, factory, harbor, house, laboratory, port, road, school, village*, etc.

Idioms

An idiom is a relatively frozen expression whose meaning does not reflect the meanings of its component parts.[5] Twenty examples of typical CE idioms are: *to have an axe to grind* "to seek personal advantage"; *to have one's back to the wall* "to be in a desperate situation"; *to jump (climb) on (aboard) the bandwagon* "to join a group that apparently will be successful", *to be beside oneself* "to be in a state of great emotional confusion"; *to kill two birds with one stone* "to achieve two aims with one action"; *to champ at the bit* "to be impatient to begin"; *in the black* "with no debts"; *in cold blood* "calmly, with no feeling of guilt"; *to miss the boat* "to let an opportunity slip by"; *to make no bones about something* "to say something frankly"; *to throw the book at somebody* "to punish somebody severely"; *to hit (take to) the bottle* "to become an alcoholic"; *to bow and scrape* "to behave in an obsequious manner"; *a busman's holiday* "a holiday on which one does the same thing as he/she does at work"; *to let the cat out of the bag* "to reveal inadvertently"; *a wild-goose chase* "a futile search"; *to keep one's chin up* "to not despair in the face of great difficulties"; *when the chips are down* "when a crisis is reached"; *the coast is clear* "there is no danger"; *the other side of the coin* "the opposite point of view":

As demonstrated in the examples just cited, some idioms allow lexical variability: *to jump* (or *climb* or *get*) *on* (or *aboard*) *the bandwagon*. Grammatical variability is normally possible: *they have—had an axe to grind*.

Some fixed expressions are called *proverbs* or *sayings*. These differ from ordinary idioms in several ways. Occasionally, their meaning can be literal or nearly literal: *an apple a day keeps the doctor away*. However, the essential difference is that they convey folk wisdom or an alleged general truth: *a bird in the hand is worth two in the bush, he who hesitates is lost, a stitch in time saves nine*, etc. Consequently, proverbs are usually complete sentences; idioms often represent parts of sentences. Lastly, proverbs are usually more frozen than idioms, that is, they allow less grammatical and lexical variability.

Lexicographers should include as many idioms as the size of their dictionaries allows. However, obsolete or rare idioms should not be entered in dictionaries of contemporary, standard English. The British learner's dictionaries cope better with idioms than American dictionaries do. For example, of the twenty idioms listed above, the LDOCE gives nineteen; the ALD gives seventeen. The two most recently published abridged American dictionaries— the *Webster's Ninth New Collegiate Dictionary* and the *American Heritage Dictionary, Second College Edition* each give only eleven.[6]

Each dictionary should explain its method of listing idioms and should adhere consistently to that method. One system, used in the *Longman*

Dictionary of English Idioms, is to alphabetize idioms according to the first noun; if there is no noun—according to the first verb; if there is no noun or verb—according to the first adjective; otherwise—according to the first adverb, etc. Note, however, that in general-use dictionaries (by contrast with specialized dictionaries of idioms) two types of idioms may receive special treatment. One type is idioms that function as nouns (e.g. *busman's holiday*, *wild-goose chase*). The other type is phrasal verbs (e.g. *give up*, *run across*, *look down on*). Some dictionaries enter such idioms as main entries, some dictionaries enter them as sub-entries (like other idioms), and some dictionaries adopt various intermediate policies.

In order to improve their treatment of idioms, especially for use by native speakers of other languages, dictionaries should pay more attention to the differences between AE, BE, and CE usage.[7] Here are several examples of such differences: *to be left holding the* (BE) *baby*—(CE) *bag*; *he/she wouldn't touch something with a* (BE) *bargepole*—(CE) *ten-foot pole*; *to lock the* (AE) *barn door*—(BE) *stable door after the horse* (AE) *is stolen*—(BE) *has bolted*; *to sweep something under the* (BE) *carpet*—(AE) *rug*; *to lead somebody a merry* (AE) *chase*—(BE) *dance*, etc.

Conclusion

We have seen that even the best contemporary dictionaries of English can improve their treatment of collocations and idioms. Such an improvement would be of special benefit for those dictionary users who are studying English as a second or foreign language.

Notes

1. Much of the material presented here is based on the book *The Lexicographic Description of English*, coauthored by this writer, Evelyn Benson, and Robert Ilson. Benjamins, forthcoming.
2. See Apresyan *et al.* and Mel'čuk *et al.* For other important discussions of collocations, see Aisenstadt and Cowie (1978, 1981), and Mackin.
3. CA collocations correspond approximately to several ECD functions such as *Oper*, *Caus*, *CausFunc*, etc.
4. EN collocations correspond approximately to the ECD function *Liqu*.
5. For a theoretical discussion of idiomaticity, see Weinreich.
6. This is, to be sure, a small, unscientific sample. Nontheless, it is sufficient to show that a difference does exist.
7. Existing general-use and specialized dictionaries have not treated this problem adequately. Among the specialized dictionaries of idioms that exist, the *Longman Dictionary of English Idioms* and Cowie *et al.* (ODCIE II) describe BE usage; Boatner *et al.* concentrates on AE usage. Attention is paid to AE–BE differences in Chapter Two of the forthcoming *Dictionary Description of English*, mentioned in note 1.

Bibliography

Aisenstadt, E. "Collocability Restrictions in Dictionaries." *ITL: Review of Applied Linguistics*, **45–46** (1979), pp. 71–74.

Apresyan, Yu. D., I. A. Mel'čuk, and A. K. Žolkovsky. "Semantics and Lexicography: Towards a New Type of Unilingual Dictionary." In *Studies in Syntax and Semantics*. Ed. F. Kiefer. Dordrecht (Holland): Reidel, 1969, pp. 1–33.

Boatner, Maxine Tull and John Edward Gates. Revised ed. edited by Adam Makkai. *A Dictionary of American Idioms*. Woodbury (N. Y.), etc.: Barrons, 1975.

Chomsky, Noam. *Aspects of the Theory of Syntax*. Cambridge (Mass.): MIT Press, 1965.

Cowie, A. P. "The Place of Illustrative Material and Collocations in the Design of a Learner's Dictionary." In *In Honour of A. S. Hornby*. Ed. Peter Strevens. Oxford: Oxford University Press, 1978, pp. 127–139.

Cowie, A. P. "The Treatment of Collocations and Idioms in Learner's Dictionaries." *Applied Linguistics*, **2**.3 (1981), pp. 223–235.

Cowie, A. P., R. Mackin, and I. R. McCaig. *Oxford Dictionary of Current Idiomatic English*. Vol. II (Phrase, Clause and Sentence Idioms). Oxford: Oxford Univ. Press, 1983.

Hornby, A. S. *Oxford Advanced Learner's Dictionary of Current English*. 3rd ed. Oxford: Oxford University Press, 1974 and 1980.

Longman Dictionary of Contemporary English. Paul Procter, Editor-in-Chief and Robert Ilson, Managing Editor. Longman, 1978 and 1981.

Longman Dictionary of English Idioms. Thomas Hill Long, Editorial Director. Harlow and London: Longman, 1979.

Mackin, Ronald. "On Collocations: 'Words Shall Be Known by the Company They Keep'." In *In Honour of A. S. Hornby*. Ed. Peter Strevens. Oxford: Oxford University Press, 1978, pp. 149–165.

Mel'čuk, I. A., L. N. Iordanskaja, and N. Arbachewsky-Jumarie. "Un Nouveau Type de dictionnaire: Le Dictionnaire explicatif et combinatoire du français contemporain." *Cahiers de lexicologie*, **38** (1981), **1,** pp. 3–34.

Weinreich, Uriel. "Problems in the Analysis of Idioms." In Uriel Weinreich, *On Semantics*. Ed. William Labov and Beatrice S. Weinreich. Philadelphia: University of Pennsylvania Press, 1980, pp. 208–264.

DEFINING THE INDEFINABLE

DWIGHT BOLINGER

Harvard University and Stanford University

Picture an overzealous gardener who broadcasts onion seed at the rate of a dozen per square inch, lets the plants grow to a tangled mass, and extracts one to describe. Its central stalk is more or less intact but its roots are torn and the resulting description, while grossly true, will forever stand in need of repair because of those missing tendrils.

Lexicography is an unnatural occupation. It consists in tearing words from their mother context and setting them in rows—carrots and onions and beetroot and salsify next to one another—with roots shorn like those of celery to make them fit side by side, in an order determined not by nature but by some obscure Phoenician sailors who traded with Greeks in the long ago.[1]* Half of the lexicographer's labor is spent repairing this damage to an infinitude of natural connections that every word in any language contracts with every other word, in a complex neural web knit densely at the center but ever more diffusely as it spreads outward. A bit of context, a synonym, a grammatical category, an etymology for remembrance' sake, and a cross-reference or two—these are the additives that accomplish the repair. But the fact that it is a repair always shows, and explains why no two dictionaries agree in their patchwork, unless they copy each other.

Undamaged definition is impossible because we know our words not as individual bits but as parts of what Pawley and Syder (1983) call lexicalized sentence stems, hundreds of thousands of them, conveniently memorized to repeat—and adapt—as the occasion arises. And also as part of an associative network involving words of similar and opposite meaning, words of similar sound, similar spelling, similar register, and similar affect. A speaker who does not command this array, as Pawley and Syder point out, does not know the language, and there is little that a dictionary can do to promote fluency beyond offering a few hints.

Any word or formative will do as a case study, but I choose the suffix *-less* because of the rather assured way in which dictionaries treat it. And also because of its historic depth, with forgotten stems like *feck-*, *hap-*, and *list-* contributing their ancient association alongside the latest nonceword to prove eternal vitality, with stem and suffix coloring one another in ways no dictionary captures quite so well as we wish it might.

(Most of the following references are to the *Oxford English Dictionary*, the *Century Dictionary*, and the Merriam Webster *Third New International*

---

* Superscript numbers are to Notes at end of article

Dictionary, abbreviated OED, C, and W3 respectively. The *Random House* and *American Heritage* dictionaries have little to say on the subject.)

A word first about the phonology. Though C states that *-less* "is applicable to any noun of which absence or destitution may be asserted", and OED says, more conservatively, "very freely attached to sbs [substantives—ed.] to form adjs [adjectives—ed.]", while W3 is simply silent on the matter, there are loose restrictions in colloquial English that conform rather closely to those of the comparative suffix *-er*, which OED explains in some detail. Venturesome speakers or writers sometimes extend *-er* beyond its normal limits (*unpleasanter*, *abstracter*), and *-less* is a shade freer still (and apparently was more so in the past, at least in writing—*resistless*, *remediless*, *husbandless*, *breakfastless*, all attested in OED), but for the most part *-less* is attached only to monosyllables or to disyllables with "light" second syllables, which contain reduced vowels without an overplus of consonants. *Skipperless*, not attested in OED, is better phonologically than *captainless*, which is attested. Forms like *card-caseless* (attested) and *drinking-glassless* (unattested) would be said only jokingly.

What concerns us more directly is meaning, and here we find, at the growing end, the literal sense of *-less* in a context of figure and ground, with "absence" applied to the figure. Thus one can have a *leafless twig* but not a *twigless leaf, a *wickless lantern* but not a *lanternless wick. The possibilities are broadly defined in the same way as the formula *X has (a) Y*: *A lantern has a wick*, **A wick has a lantern*. *A hand has a finger* thus predicts *a fingerless hand*, whereas **An arm has a finger* predicts *a fingerless arm. More narrowly, if a subpart is not apt to be conceived as figure—it may, for example, be too readily assimilated into the ground—it is not apt to take *-less*: we have *yolkless eggs* but not *whiteless eggs, and *warless world* makes a better gestalt than ?*peaceless world* (though OED attests *peaceless*). Thus *-less* is a shade more demanding of a sharp figure-ground relationship than is *have*. Given that relationship we are free to invent such unattested (by OED) forms as *moatless castle*, *mittenless hand*, *nounless clause*, *titless udder*, *zipperless jacket*, *doctorless clinic*, plus equally well-formed expressions that OED would probably regard as nonce, as in *This is the first hashless meal I've had in a week*.

That much is basic, and the association of adjective and noun is often so close that the noun is virtually presupposed by the adjective: *oarless* (*boat*), *motherless* (*child*), *rimless* (*glasses*, *tire*), *chinless* (*face*, *jaw*). This is coupled with a considerable amount of stereotyping. Though one might have a *horseless corral*, *horseless carriage* is the usual association, and similarly *strapless gown*, *beltless maxi*, *treeless plain*, *childless couple* (*marriage*, *family*— but **childless society* is a bad gestalt), *landless peasant* (possessors are normally ground), *stainless steel*, *scoreless game*, *sleepless night*.

A clue to some of the grosser aspects of meaning is found in the attempts of dictionaries to define by synonym or antonym. C states that *-less* adjectives are "usually equivalent to the negative *un-* prefixed to an adjective in *-ful*, *-y*, *-ing*, or *-ed*, as *unhopeful*, *unwitty*, *unending*, *unmatched*". First, *-ful* adjectives are almost without exception gradable; the comparison readily applies: *very dreadful*, *youthful*, *playful*, *tearful*, *insightful*, *grateful* (the phrase *r-ful and r-less* *dialects*, with ungradable *r-ful*, was probably facetious to begin with). Adjectives in *-less*, though quite often gradable (*very fearless, tactless, useless*), are typically ungradable, either because what is missing must be totally missing if it is missing at all (**very collarless, supperless, sugarless, legless*), or because the adjective represents an ungradable extreme like *perfect* and *unique* (**very countless, *very ceaseless, *very deathless, ?very merciless*). Related to this is the fact that *-less* is attached to both concrete and abstract nouns, the former resulting in words that are almost by definition ungradable, whereas *-ful* is almost uniformly attached to abstract nouns (an exception such as *manful* has *man* in an abstract sense). And even when *-ful* and *-less* are attached to the same noun, the result is seldom a good antonymic pair. *Useful* and *useless* might qualify, as would *harmful* and *harmless, cheerful* and *cheerless* (applied to "place" but not to "person"). But whereas *graceful* leans in the direction of movement, *graceless* leans toward manner and attitude. *Soulful* is almost restricted to "look" ("eyes", etc.), *soulless* applies to what is unfeeling generally. Even *sinful* and *sinless* do not quite match—a *sinless world* is a world in which there is no sin; a *sinful world* is a world that commits sin. And when those who work with the blind needed an antonym for *sightless* they did not resort to *sightful* but to *sighted*.

What gives the several flavors to *-less* adjectives is the absolute vanishing of the figure from the ground. At the crudest level this produces the ungradable adjectives based mostly on concrete nouns. But it generates two main outgrowths found mostly with abstract nouns (though with a great deal of metaphorical extension from concrete nouns) which, depending on whether the noun designates an undesirable figure or a desirable one, can be labeled "freedom" and "deprivation". Add "absoluteness" to this and you tend to get adjectives that lean toward the extreme of the scale.

Deprivation seems to involve the principle of the "aching void". A large family of *-less* adjectives are typified by *hopeless*—they are negatively valued and cluster about such meanings as dejection, disorientation, and abandonment: *homeless, motherless, anchorless, rudderless, aimless, comfortless, loveless, joyless, meaningless, helpless, spiritless, feckless, hapless, remediless*. A related cluster is tied to "futility": *useless, fruitless, pointless, profitless, worthless*. Nearby are "weakness", "apathy", "awkwardness', "dulness", and other undesirable states, all expressed in a relatively extreme degree: *powerless, wordless, listless, graceless, tasteless, lifeless, senseless, luckless*. The sense of extremity can be seen by comparing *luckless* with its synonym *unlucky*. We say *He was unlucky in that game; luckless* is "permanently unlucky", and would not be used in that context. A number of *-less* words—mostly but not exclusively deverbal—refer to some extreme of measurement: *countless, numberless, measureless, fathomless, depthless, plumbless*. Even ungradable *-less* adjectives tend to be somewhat hyperbolic. We say *He was barefoot* or *unshod* but less likely *shoeless*, which would be a more extreme state of discalcement, perhaps that of not owning a pair. *To go to bed supperless* is a worse state of privation than *to go to bed without supper*—the latter would be more compatible with freedom to get up at 1 a.m. for a snack. *Baseless* and *groundless* are more potent than *unfounded, deathless* is so more than *undying, matchless* more so than *unmatched.* One who is *speechless* is thunderstruck, one who is *wordless* confronts the ineffable. To stand *motionless* is a more rigid pose than to stand *still* or *unmoving.* A *windowless house* is more than without windows: it is blind.

Other *-less* words are similarly stereotyped in a hyperbolic sense: *penniless* is matched only by *destitute* (*moneyless* is not fixed in this way), *faceless* is the extreme of anonymity. Of course stereotyping can work in reverse, by overuse: *doubtless* is the weakest member of the series *doubtless, no doubt, undoubtedly, without doubt, without a doubt, without a shadow of a doubt.*

The potency of the aching void makes *-less* propitious for words used to denigrate: *witless, brainless, mindless, godless, mannerless, shiftless, spineless, merciless, heartless, shapeless, lawless, toothless, reckless, thoughtless, shame-less.* (The curious near-synonymy with *shameful* results from "having no sense of shame" versus "crying shame upon".)

The positively-valued adjectives are mostly the ones whose nouns (or occasionally verbs) designate something undesirable, whence the meaning "free from": *ageless, blameless, dauntless, fearless, fadeless, faultless, guileless, peerless, spotless, scatheless, tireless.* Though there are weaker members of the set (*harmless, odorless, painless*) and of course many more that are ungradable (*warless, crimeless, stainless*), a high proportion of these adjectives are as strongly positive as those cited earlier are strongly negative. In this respect W3 and also the *Longman New Universal Dictionary* are misleading in the part corresponding to W3's definition 3: "unable or lacking power to be acted upon or to act (in a specified way)—in adjectives formed from verbs", with examples *resistless, dauntless, quenchless, tireless, fadeless, ceaseless.* "Lacking power" is precisely the opposite of what these adjectives imply, which is "too powerful to be resisted", "too powerful to be daunted", etc. One has or lacks power to act, not to be acted upon; by trying to cram too much in a single phrase the definition falsifies the majority of deverbal *-less* adjectives. (A secondary sense of *resistless* does fit: "unable to resist" rather than "too powerful to be resisted".) Again we find that some ungradable adjectives show the same tendency toward extremes as happened with the ungradables among the negatively-valued examples cited earlier. So a *smokeless industry*[2] is one that has no relationship with smoke (such as an electronics firm or a publishing house), whereas a *smoke-free industry* may be one that controls its emissions.

The strongly evaluative overtones of *-less* adjectives make them a natural choice for writing—and to a lesser extent speech—that lays some claim to lyricism, and authors seem to enjoy playing with the suffix. OED cites W. H. Hudson's *peaceful gnatless days.* There is an airy intensity about phrases like *shoreless sea, stormless sky, shadowless pond, brimless cup, faithless lover, endless desire, deathless affection, nameless dread, relentless hatred, seamless web, spaceless infinity, remoreseless enemy, windless afternoon.* Metaphorical transfers are common: *breathless* for "eager", *faceless* for "anonymous", *brainless* for "stupid". The poetic sweep of many *-less* words makes them unsuitable for humdrum settings. One may readily say *The expedition crossed a grassless plain* but not **Our neighbor has a grassless back yard.* This may also explain why some resist predicate position: *How far can you get in an oarless boat?* is normal, but *?The boat was oarless* is odd; we prefer *The boat had no* *oars*. What *-less* accomplishes is a transformation of *to have no* or *to be without* to a form that is syntactically and prosodically suitable for attributive position, which in turn lends the "characterizing" quality of that position, its solidity and permanence (see Bolinger, 1967). A *-less* adjective plus a noun is a picture frozen in place, and the freest use of *-less* is to form nonce words grouped in just such a collective still life: *If I were on a mountaintop, my wish would be to look down upon an autoless landscape, out to a rigless[3] sea, and up to a planeless sky*.

Much more could be said, but this account of sinuosities is enough to show how much we destroy when we define. Some destruction is inevitable, for a dictionary must limit its aims. As Lakoff (1973) says, "The purpose of a dictionary . . . is to fill in what the speaker cannot be expected to know already"—to which we must add, "and also to serve as a reminder of forgotten knowledge and an organizer of diffuse knowledge". To do the best within these limitations requires not only attention to logic and precision but sensitivity to affect. In that respect the most satisfactory definition of *-less* in the unabridged dictionaries[4] I have in front of me is from the shortest, the *Longman Dictionary of Contemporary English*. It employs five simple equivalents: (1) "lacking", which covers the negatively-valued "deprivation" senses; (2) "free from", which covers the positively valued senses; (3) "without", which takes care of the most literal cases; and (4) "beyond" and (5) "that never . . . s or that cannot be . . . ed", which take care of power and hyperbole. By contrast, the W3 definition not only imputes powerlessness where it should impute power, but chooses as example of the "free from" sense the word *doubtless*, which as we saw earlier is the least free from doubt of all the sentence adverbials that incorporate *doubt*. Many things can misrepresent a meaning, including an excess of erudition.

Editorial Notes

1. Referring to the development of the alphabet by the Greeks after its invention by the Phoenicians. (*Ed.*)
2. The expression *smokestack industries* is now current in American English to refer to traditional heavy industries (with or without smokestacks) such as the manufacture of steel or motor-cars. (*Ed.*)
3. The reference here is to off-shore *oil-rigs*. (*Ed.*)
4. That is, dictionaries (of any size) not shortened from longer ones. (*Ed.*)

References

Bolinger, D. "Adjectives in English: attribution and predication" in *Lingua* **18:** 1–34, 1967.
Lakoff, R. "Lexicography and generative grammar II: context and connotation in the dictionary" in *Annals of the New York Academy of Sciences* Vol. 211, 8 June 1973.
Pawley, A. and F. Syder "Two puzzles for linguistic theory: nativelike selection and nativelike fluency" in *Language and Communication*. Longman, 1983.
[Cf. Rossner's Appendix, this volume—ed.]

USAGE NOTES IN DICTIONARIES: THE NEEDS OF THE LEARNER AND THE NATIVE SPEAKER

JANET WHITCUT
Longman Group Ltd

The core of any dictionary entry is the "denotational meaning": in a monolingual dictionary a substitutable paraphrase of the headword; in a bilingual dictionary, a translation. Whatever else it does, any dictionary must tell us either that *mud* is "dust or earth mixed with water" or that *mud* is "boue".

But lexicographic tradition provides conventionalized ways of saying a great deal more than this about a word. We show, perhaps, the points at which a long word may best be broken at a line ending:

(1) *ob.ser.vance*

We show variant spellings:

(2) *depersonalize, -ise*   *sceptic* or US *skeptic*

We give at least one recommended pronunciation, and perhaps one or more permissible variants, in the form of either a phonetic transcription or a version in "respelling":

(3) *harass* /'hærəs, hə'ræs/   *ragwort* /'rag,wuht/

At this point, following the traditional ordering, we state the "part of speech"; either giving the possibilities one at a time, or showing them all together:

(4) *poison . . . n & vt*

Any irregular inflections usually follow:

(5) *mow . . . v mown* or *mowed*

We have still not reached the denotational meaning, because at this point, if at all, comes such information as "capitalization":

(6) *pop art . . .* often cap *P&A*

and "labels" of time, place, level of formality, and the like:

(7) *eftsoons . . .* (archaic) *bairn . . .* (chiefly Scot)
booze . . . (informal) *ain't . . .* (nonstandard)

and perhaps, immediately before the meaning, a specification of the subject of a verb or the noun typically modified by an adjective:

(8) *serve . . .* (of a male animal) to copulate with
lean . . . (of meat) without much fat

Now at last comes the core definition. We have not done with the additional matter, though, because if the definition is of a transitive verb an "object specification" may here follow or be interpolated:

(9)   *contract* . . . to catch (an illness)
bond . . . to overlap (e.g. bricks) for solidity of construction

The conventions of ordering are less rigid at this point, but next will probably come any example sentences:

(10)   *discolour* . . . to change in colour for the worse: *teeth discoloured by heavy smoking*

and any information about collocation and idiom:

(11)   *acquiesce* . . . to submit or comply tacitly or passively—often + *in*
kilter . . . good working order—chiefly in the phrase *out of kilter*
bandwagon . . . a party or cause that attracts followers by its timeliness or momentum—*jump/climb on the bandwagon* . . .

If the etymology has not, as in some dictionaries, immediately followed the part of speech, it comes at the end, before or after the idioms and any "run-on" formations:

(12)   *internal* . . . [L *internus*; akin to L *inter* between](13)—   *internally adv*

So much for the entry structure that has been handed down to us. At first blush it looks coherent and impressive enough, as if it must cover anything anyone could possibly want to say about the behaviour of a word. Yet as any experienced lexicographer knows, the material upon which we work is as disparate, intractable, and fuzzy as the universe itself, not always lending itself to this procrustean treatment. There is often a good deal more that needs to be said, and Usage notes, those little paragraphs at the end of dictionary entries, are one useful way of saying it.

They are not the only way. A historically-ordered dictionary tells the reader, for instance, simply by the way it is ordered which is the oldest sense or the earliest homograph of a word, and may reinforce this by the use of dated citations; by contrast a frequency-ordered dictionary makes a similar implicit statement about frequency. In the former, a *fowl* is first any kind of bird: in the latter it is first a domestic hen. Similarly, though it is an important function of Usage notes to describe syntax, there are other ways of describing it. The basic fact of verb transitivity is dealt with, though rather too simplistically, in most native-speaker dictionaries at the part-of-speech stage, by the conventional *vt* or *vi*. Good monolingual dictionaries for the foreign learner convey a great deal more syntactic information than this in the form of grammatical codes or other bracketed material before the definition, or at individual senses: it should not need an elaborate Usage paragraph to tell us that *justice* is a mass noun when it's a quality but a count noun when it's a judge.

At almost any point of the conventional entry structure, however, there may be something extra to be said. The dictionary shows that *-ize* verbs such as *depersonalize* have a variant spelling *-ise*, but a Usage paragraph, probably at the suffix *-ize*, can usefully discuss the relative frequency of *-ize* and *-ise* in British and in American English, and perhaps warn people against overdoing the *-ize* spelling to produce *exercize* and *advertize*. The dictionary, whose primary duty is to describe, shows two pronunciations at *harass*, but a Usage note may usefully comment that the incoming American /həˈræs/ makes some British hackles rise. The dictionary gives the past participle of *mow* as either *mown* or *mowed*, but a note is needed to explain that while *mowed* is usual in verbal use (she's *mowed* the lawn) *mown* is the usual attributive adjective (new-*mown* hay). The historically-ordered dictionary gives first for *awful* the sense connected with *awe*, but a note may discuss whether this is still the only "proper" meaning, or indeed a viable meaning at all.

Examples can show how a word can be used, but not how it can't. The device of subject or object specification, on the other hand, does impose one sort of restriction on use: it tells us that *contract* can replace *catch* only when the object is an illness, not when it is a ball or a train. When things get more complicated than this, a Usage note is useful, to explain perhaps that art is *Islamic* but people *Muslim*. But the three chief functions of Usage notes are to elaborate upon the syntax of words, more fully than is possible for the native-speaker dictionary with its simple part-of-speech system, or even for the monolingual foreign learner's dictionary with its more detailed grammatical information; to discuss neologisms and disputed use; and to overcome the intransigence of alphabetical ordering by relating one lexical item to another.

The native-speaker's interest in usage is mainly over its disputed areas. In the area of syntax, are the data-processing people justified in treating *data* as a singular noun? Is "between you and *I*" to be changed to "between you and *me*"? Are we to allow the British regionalism of "I want this *cleaning*" or to correct it to "I want this *cleaned*"? Is "if it *were*" better than "if it *was*"? Should it be "everyone must do *his* best", or "*his or her* best", or "*their best*"?

Native speakers who worry at all about English subscribe to a certain set of deeply-entrenched shibboleths on the subject, implanted in them and their forebears by generations of teachers. It is a matter of etiquette, rather like table manners. The alert writer of Usage material must begin by identifying these causes célèbres, which is fairly easily done since they are the subject of continual letters to the BBC and to the serious newspapers, and must then decide what to do about them, since something has to be said. The responsible attitude is to point out objectively the existence of the shibboleth, discuss where appropriate its rationale, and give advice. Thus, one may properly say that some people still think there should not be more than two *alternatives*, because the word is derived from the Latin *alter* = "the other of two"; but that today it is legitimate in good writing to speak of several *alternatives*. A dictum of this kind inspires more confidence if it can be accompanied by citations from the writing of respected authors: T. E. Lawrence wrote of "our three *alternatives*". Samuel Richardson contravened the shibboleth against using *aggravate* to mean "annoy", by writing "to *aggravate* her parents". Charles Darwin used *like* as a conjunction, writing "few have observed *like* you have done". Shakespeare used dangling participles, as in "*Sitting* within my orchard, a serpent stung me." Since there is no Academy to control English, the appeal to such precedents has a rather powerful effect, though one should not carry the practice too far because one may sometimes have to overrule, so to speak, the precedents: a warning against writing the chiefly British *different to* can be accompanied both by a quotation such as this from Fielding, "It's quite a *different* thing within *to* what it is without", and by the advice that, nevertheless, *different from* is the safest choice for the 1980's.

These are some of the old chestnuts of Usage material. Readers who go beyond these appear to be chiefly concerned, not so much with plainly censured items such as *ain't* or "we *was*" as with novelty of any kind, about which they mind instinctively: those who do not like a sum of money to be called "twelve *pee*" are mostly too old to have been warned against the expression by their teachers, since the new penny came in only in 1971. People dislike the use of old words in new senses, so that those who hate the use of *disinterested* to mean "uninterested" are sometimes mollified when they learn that this is a return to an older meaning than the preferred "altruistic". People dislike specialist jargon such as *interface* or *parameter* when it crops up in nonspecialist situations; and they complain about the word *situation* itself, particularly in the cliché phrase *ongoing situation*, as also about *this day and age*, *at the end of the day*, *at this point in time*, and *you name it*. Finally, the more cantakerous defenders of British English complain about such incoming Americanisms as they can identify: about the use of *hopefully* as a sentence adverb, "*Hopefully*, we'll be there in an hour"; about pronunciations such as *ha*RASS and RE*search*; about the use of *loan* for *lend* and *around* for *approximately*. A dictionary should mention as many as possible of these things in one way or another, either by a Usage note or where appropriate by a label such as "chiefly American".

The foreign learner's problems over "correctness" are very different. A foreigner has no natural predisposition in favour of "between you and *I*", and come to that has probably never even heard *ain't* or "we *was*". The areas of concern for the learner are those parts of usage that are not disputed at all: such problems as the plurality of *news*, which looks like a plural but isn't; the verb patterns of speech verbs (you can *tell* me but not *say* me); when not to use *the*; whether one can ever use a future tense after *if*; when to say *of* (the table's leg or the leg *of* the table); and which prepositions go with which words. In addition, there are that host of further difficulties that arise from "interference error", the drawing of mistaken analogies from the learner's own mother tongue. The German learner must be warned against saying "a *bit* money", and both French and German learners against saying "*since* three weeks". A good many of these well-known pedagogical hazards are covered anyway in a good foreigners' dictionary if you look at the small print: *news* will be marked as an uncountable (singular) noun, and the list of permissible objects for *say* does not include a person. But even these may need to be made more explicit, and others, such as *the* and "a *bit* money", can be handled only in a Usage note.

As for neologism and cliché, the foreigner must triumphantly master *interface* and *you name it* before attaining the further sophistication needed to discard them, so no comment is needed.

When it comes to the relationships between lexical items, foreigners and native speakers have many interests in common. Antonyms (*underhand* and *aboveboard*) are equally useful to both groups, and if intelligently introduced are a great help in distinguishing senses: one sense of *right* means "not *wrong*", another means "not *left*". Comparisons between related words are also generally useful: *apogee*—compare *perigee*, and *bass*—compare *treble*. Both groups can profit by straight synonymies (*puma* is another word for *cougar*) and also by synonym essays that discuss a related cluster of words, although the foreigner's need will usually be at a simpler level than the native's: *coast/beach/shore/seaside* as against *transient/evanescent/ephemeral/fleeting*. Here, as so often in language learning, the foreigner is perhaps grappling with the problem of making a new distinction not recognized by his or her mother tongue, which may have only one word for *coast* and *shore*. Some synonym essays for both foreigner and native can usefully be quite encyclopaedic, discussing "things" as well as "words"; we don't all know the crucial differences between a *hydrofoil* and a *hovercraft*, and unless the two words have been conscientiously defined in contrast with each other and linked by a cross-reference, we may not find out those differences without a synonym essay. The foreigner is here on a level footing with the native if *hydrofoil* and *hovercraft* are easily translatable into his or her mother tongue.

Malapropisms, again, are useful to both groups, in so far as the foreigner's vocabulary is large enough for the malapropism to arise: you don't confuse *mitigate* with *militate* or *formication* with *fornication* unless you know at least one of the words. The lexicographer is treading on delicate ground here, though, in deciding where malapropism stops: if nobody has ever confused *formication* with *fornication* it seems hardly worth telling them not to, but if too many people have confused them the thing becomes almost legitimate; we have to show *flout* as one sense of *flaunt* (he *flaunted* the rules) and *imply* as one sense of *infer* (her manner *inferred* that she was sorry) however much we circumscribe such usages with warning labels such as "nonstandard".

Both learners and natives have problems of collocation, though not the same problems. The native's intuition handles correctly the collocational problems of what you *do* and what you *make* (*do* business or a favour, *make* love or war) and of *near* and *close* (the *near* future, but a *close* friend) both of which deserve a Usage note in the foreigner's dictionary. The native is interested in prepositions where their collocation is in dispute (is it *in* or *under* the circumstances, is it compared *to* or compared *with*?) but has apparently no difficulty in handling the particular sort of collocation involved in building phrasal verbs properly, though perhaps disliking them when they have been built; many British speakers find *check up on* malevolently transatlantic. The native as well as the foreigner, when attempting to write in an unfamiliar formal register, makes mistakes with the prepositional collocations that belong to that register. A recent crop of Fifth-form history essays produced "Charles's dislike *to* Lutheranism" and "Russia mobilized in support *for* Serbia", which means that *dislike* should be provided with a collocating *of* in the native-speaker dictionary, and *in support of* shown as a collocational unit. There is no need to tell natives, however, that it's *by* mistake but *on* purpose.

Varieties of English, or at least some broad British–American distinctions, are interesting to both natives and advanced learners; and the subject can be discussed more delicately in Usage notes than in the simple nationality labels, adequate though these are for saying that Americans use *fall* as well as World-English *autumn*, or that the British and the Americans mean something different by a *cot* or by *wash up*. But when is a *holiday* a *vacation*? What kind of things do the British and the Americans respectively *rent*, and what do they *hire*?

Finally, the advanced learner just as much as the native needs some advice on how to avoid ambiguity when writing formal prose: perhaps on the dangers of using *which* to refer to a whole clause. Does "she crashed the car, *which* was expensive" contain a comment on the expense of the car or of the crash? And since *as* can mean either "while" or "because", a sentence such as "*As* Anne was working, I bathed the baby" has two possible meanings. Such problems affect anyone learning to write either their own or a new language in a register more structured than that of casual speech.

Everything up to this point can and should be dealt with in the dictionary, either at the core of the formal entry structure or, by various devices of which the Usage paragraph is merely one, round its edges. It is necessary now to remind ourselves of what a dictionary is, and of the ways in which its Usage content must inevitably differ from that of a free-ranging Usage book that is not a dictionary. There is one whole kind of problem which the dictionary Usage note need not tackle, but which the Usage book must; and one other kind which the dictionary Usage note cannot tackle, but which the Usage book can.

As regards the first kind of problem, a dictionary Usage note has got a dictionary there already, with its spelling, its definitions, and all the rest of the paraphernalia. Though it may be appropriate to comment on any of these things, one is not required to say what they actually are, because the dictionary says so. Thus, while the dictionary Usage note at *mitigate* may say something like "Not to be confused with *militate*", the Usage book will give the definitions: "*Mitigate* means make less bad, *militate* means have significant effect".

The second problem is that a dictionary Usage note has to be put at a headword in the dictionary. One can transcend alphabetical order by cross-reference between words, as from each of a group of words discussed as synonyms to a central synonym essay at one of them. But the dictionary offers no obvious place for discussing topics of interest which go beyond the word, such as punctuation problems and sequence of tenses, or which apply to too many words, such as verb and pronoun concord after group nouns [Cf Lamy, this volume, note 7—ed.]. By fudging it a bit one can perhaps discuss some of these matters at the headword which is their grammatical name: appending, for instance, essays on the justifiability of dangling participles and split infinitives at *dangling participle* and *split infinitive*. There is a certain philosophical oddity about this practice, since *dangling participle* is not itself a "dangling participle"; but we may be willing to live with this. For that matter, *hydrofoil* isn't a hydrofoil. We ought to be far more worried, though, by the thousand-dollar question which should be engraved in marble over every lexicographer's desk: "But How Will They Know Where To Look It Up?"

LEXICOGRAPHIC EVIDENCE

JOHN SINCLAIR

University of Birmingham

The main sources of lexicographic evidence are, probably in order of popularity:

1. Other dictionaries
2. Introspection
3. Observation of language in use.

I have been asked to concentrate on the third of these, so the emphasis of this paper is the wish of the Editor. But the subject as a whole merits a brief general discussion.

The three categories of evidence listed above are roughly the same three as would be invoked for any enterprise in descriptive linguistics.

1. Received and documented description of the language
2. Native speaker introspection
3. Text.

The second type should be sub-divided:

2a. Informant testing
2b. Introspection by the linguist.

Received Description

The great value of received description is that the information is already organized. Language change is not so rapid that descriptions go out of date quickly, and from decade to decade we must assume that most existing work is valid and accurate. A synthesis of good practice, with obvious corrections and updatings, should produce a reliable dictionary fairly quickly.

The disadvantages of reliance upon existing lexicography are:

(a) It is difficult to know when a word or a usage lapses; hence for a contemporary record the evidence of existing dictionaries is misleading.
(b) Structural mistakes in an entry are difficult to detect, since they only become noticeable when compiling starts from scratch.
(c) New developments in linguistic description, for example pragmatic information, cannot easily be fitted into established lexicographic formats or indeed into the whole conceptual background of lexicography. Received information cannot be shaken free of its theoretical origins.

Where good evidence is available from other sources, existing dictionaries are very helpful as a check on coverage, because the bigger ones are repositories of a very large amount of information. As a general rule, though, a form or a meaning should not be incorporated in a new compilation unless it is independently confirmed. The operation of this rule would gradually rid dictionaries of two types of red herring:

(a) Forms and/or meanings which have lapsed into disuse. For a contemporary dictionary this leaves space for newcomers or for further information about the modern language; for a historical dictionary this will help the dating of language change.

(b) Forms and/or meanings which are constructs of lexicography, and which do not really exist, in the sense that there is no textual evidence for them. The line between what is possible and what is reasonably natural is not easy to draw, and it would constitute a diversion in this paper to explore it in any detail (see Sinclair, 1984). But lexicographers should be scrupulous in extirpating these items.

Introspection

Informant testing, whether formal or informal, produces some useful evidence. The informal type is very common and usually gives rise to a lively, if rarely resolved, discussion. More formal investigation is limited because of the time it takes, and needs to be carefully prepared and conducted. It is unlikely to become a major source of lexicographic evidence.

The special case of the lexicographer being his own informant is worth special consideration. It has been fashionable among grammarians for many years now to introspect and to trust their intuitions about structure; why should not vocabulary be investigated in the same way?

The problem about all kinds of introspection is that it does not give evidence about usage. The informant will not be able to distinguish among various kinds of language patterning—psychological associations, semantic groupings, etc. Actual usage plays a very minor role in one's consciousness of language and one would be recording largely ideas about language rather than facts of it. Ultimately, however, the lexicographic decisions will be personal evaluations by the lexicographer, giving due consideration to all the evidence that he has amassed. Personal introspection will inevitably play a big part at that point, being inextricable from all the other factors that bear on a decision. This seems to be the most favourable point for the operation of introspection—in evaluating evidence rather than creating it.

Language in Use

I have thus suggested that both the evidence of secondary sources and the evidence of introspection should be brought in at a late stage in the process of compilation. It follows that the initial evidence should always be of the third type—from the observation of language in use.

Here again I would like to make a distinction between two sub-types:

3a. citation of instances
3b. concordancing of texts.

The first sub-type is the cornerstone of traditional lexicography. Citations, frequently from authoritative sources, formed the basis of Dr Johnson's evidence, and established a central principle in lexicography. The OED "worked a revolution in the art of lexicography" by having as its basis "a collection of some five millions of excerpts from English literature", which "collection of evidence—it is represented by a selection of about 1,800,000 quotations actually printed—could form the only possible foundation for...the work" (Preface, 1933).

The Historical Introduction to OED speaks with feeling about both the importance and the capriciousness of the evidence thus gathered by citation of instances. "Johnson and Richardson had been selective in the material they assembled, and obviously some kind of selection would be imposed by practical limits, however wide the actual range might be. This was a point on which control was difficult; the one safeguard was that the care and judgement of some readers would make up for the possible deficiencies of others."

At the time when OED was being planned and produced, the gathering of individual instances selected by a wide variety of voluntary readers was probably the best available method of amassing evidence, and for any dictionary with the historical scope of OED it may still be necessary to use this method in part, despite its unreliability. However, for most lexicographic purposes it is now possible to use the organizing power of modern computers to establish new principles and standards in the gathering of citational evidence. This is type (3b) above—the complete concordancing of a representative corpus of texts.

The selection process becomes a selection of texts for the corpus, not instances for a dictionary. Once it is decided to include a text, then all the instances of all the words constitute the evidence.

The technique of creating a corpus for linguistic study is becoming more and more important as the computers become capable of processing longer and longer texts, and of increasing the sophistication of the processing. Linguistic detail—the sort of consideration that would apply in the selection of instances—is absent from the criteria, which tend towards the sociolinguistic. A clear account of the selection criteria and procedures for the Brown corpus of 1 m words, paralleled by the LOB corpus, can be found in Hofland & Johannson (1982), and for the Birmingham Collection of English Texts, of which the working corpus is 7.3 m words, there is a description in Renouf (1984). The latter paper also deals with the creation of a specialized corpus of 1 m words, which contrasts in its structure with the Jiaotong corpus of scientific texts (JDEST), also 1 m words and structured by analogy with the Brown method (see Yang, 1984). More specialized corpora on various principles are in various stages of planning and creation, and one can confidently predict a period of great activity in this field, fuelling the lexicography of the nineties and beyond.

Given a corpus in machine-readable form, the next stage is to derive some basic information from it. The simplest computer access to a text is to regard it as a linear string of "characters". Each character corresponds to a key on the keyboard, so the wordspace character can be used to define a word, rather crudely, and the words so defined can be counted and arranged in various ways. At this stage a "word" is any string of characters with a wordspace on either side, so *boy* and *boys*, and *come, comes, came* are all different "words".

There is a lot to be learned about a language from the study of it in this simple format. Most studies leap ahead and group the crude "words" according to simple notions of meaning, instead of deriving as much information as possible from each stage in the developing sophistication of description. This crude notion of a basic linguistic unit I shall call a word *form*; it is one of the absolutes in the written language—a string of letters with space on either side.

When we talk of "the word *come*", meaning *come* or *comes* or *coming* or *came*, I would like to use the term *lemma*. So the initial statement often found in dictionaries, e.g.

come (kʌm) *vb* **comes, com + ing, came, come**

is an expression of the relationship between the lemma and its forms.

Lists of forms are commonly prepared in alphabetical order (with frequencies) or in frequency order, and sometimes reversed alphabetical order. Another valuable listing is the order of appearance of words in a text, with their frequencies again. This information can then be related to the lemmas; but problems begin to arise, since a lemma is not obvious to a computer.

The machine can simply be painstakingly told, lemma by lemma, how each lemma relates to the word forms in the texts, as in Harris (forthcoming). Or some automatic routine can be devised which should with reasonable accuracy group the forms into lemmas, and, most importantly, should present any problem cases to the researcher.

Lemmatization looks fairly straightforward, but is actually a matter of subjective judgement by the researcher. There are thousands of decisions to be taken. But when it is done, even in a provisional fashion, then there is a new branch of study available—the interrelationships of a lemma and its forms.

This is a valuable study for lexicographers, because there is a close similarity between a "headword" and its inflected and derived forms, and a lemma, in a dictionary. The question of homographs becomes interesting, for example, if one abandons etymological arguments. If two words, historically distinct, have fallen together so that there is just no physical distinction between them, what contemporary arguments can be used for separating them?

Another interesting question in this area is how it is decided what the physical form of a lemma should be. Traditionally the "base", or uninflected, form is used even when that form is hardly ever found on its own, or hardly ever found at all. But a case could be made for any of a number of alternatives, for example that the most frequently-encountered form should be used for the lemma, and the first-stage evidence from the computer can provide a good basis for planning new methods of access to the word-forms of the language.

Also available at this stage are concordances where citations of a word-form are listed. The quality of evidence about the language which can be provided by concordances is quite superior to any other method; once lexicography takes full advantage of this evidence, it will be impossible to go back to a reliance on pre-computational techniques. This is an area where the computer has opened up new horizons, which we are just beginning to glimpse.

Automatic concordancing of texts has been an established facility for many years now, and for some special studies manual or automatic concordances, e.g. to the Bible or Shakespeare, have been used. The early efforts concentrated on established literature, so that quotations and allusions could be located, and figures of speech could be studied; there was no interest in sampling the everyday language. Indeed, the size of the text samples needed is still quite daunting despite the most modern hardware and software provision.

Let us consider some of the factors affecting the shape and utility of concordances:

(a) Whether the concordance is selective or exhaustive. The ability to be exhaustive is one of the principal features of a concordance, because it can claim to present all the available information, and is clearly superior to a list of selective citations where there are no strict rules about selection. But there will be circumstances where some selection has to be made, and the principles of selection will be of the greatest importance. At present the only need for selection is in the case of the very commonest words in very long texts. The pattern of word-occurrence in texts means that for any reasonably long text, there are some words that occur too often, and some that do not occur enough. Consequently there is only a central set of words for which the evidence is both comprehensive and convenient. So the question of selection of citations can be resolved by two principles:
  (i) selection is only made when the number of instances becomes quite unmanageable otherwise
  (ii) the criteria for selection must be very carefully worked out.

(b) Specification of the whole citation. The almost universal format for concordances is the so-called KWIC (Key Word in Context), where the length of the citation is determined by the width of a bale of computer paper; the key word is in the middle. This format is fairly generally useful, but for some linguistic study of some words, it is not adequate, and more flexible formats must be devised. Specification of a citation could be by character count (as in KWIC), or word count, or by finding punctuation marks to identify sentences—or by a whole range of more sophisticated linguistic criteria.

(c) Ordering of citations. Where there are tens, hundreds or thousands of citations of a word-form it is useful to consider how they may be listed. The simplest method is text order, but for some purposes a listing in alphabetical order of the word following the keyword can be helpful, and for other purposes an ordering by the preceding word can be helpful. And sometimes both. Whichever method is chosen highlights some patterns for the eye, and obscures others.

This work is still in its crude early stages, and it is to be hoped that research will gradually improve access to the evidence that is required. Criteria for evaluating citations are urgently required, closely followed by criteria for estimating the optimum length of a given citation.

Here is a brief example of the kind of evidence that an exhaustive concordance provides; the word chosen is *decline* and its associated forms *declension*, *declines*, *declining*. Their occurrence in a general corpus of 7.3 million words is

decline	122
declined	76
declining	38
declines	9
declension	0 (total 245)

Observations from the corpus will be compared with the treatment afforded to the words in Collins' English Dictionary (CED). (I have chosen CED not as a suitable target for criticism but because I think it is the most reliable example of current lexicography in its field.)

CED gives an entry for *declension* with three distinct meanings, and a number of other forms which are not in the corpus; some of them seem unlikely starters for any corpus.

headwords	*derived forms*
declinate	declinable
declination	decliner
declinometer	declensional
	declensionally
	declinational

A word must occur to remain in the language, and therefore to be the concern of lexicographers of the contemporary language. So a word which does not occur at all in over 7 m words of general current English does not have a strong claim to be in any dictionary of it. But we must not, at present, be too rigidly guided by occurrence and frequency statistics. We should always remember that even the multi-million word samples are tiny compared to the amount of language produced in even a smallish community; so an occurrence of zero or close to zero may be just a quirk of the sampling, and a dictionary which aims to be comprehensive will have to scan hundreds of millions of words.

The problem for the lexicographer is that word formation rules are highly productive, and only the evidence of text is likely to control what is otherwise a monstrous list of forms that follow the rules, but do not, as far as we know, exist in text. Evidence from any one corpus will have an arbitrary quality, but it will also be definite on points like these.

Research will in due course offer guidelines which will gradually improve the choice of texts, sampling methods, processing of evidence and application of the results to lexicography. Until then we must use the evidence with care; but we must use it.

Words like *declension* and *declinate* may follow a different pattern associated with technical language (Roe, 1977; Phillips, 1983). Many words and phrases are rare in a general sample of texts but very frequent indeed in certain specific texts. Most vocabulary gives indications of this trend but technical language shows it in an extreme form; presumably *declension* is a fairly common word in a Latin grammar.

The full entry for *decline* in CED is given in Fig. 5 below. CED offers two word classes: *vb.* for senses 1–5, and *n.* for 6–9. The sequence *vb.–n.* is a significant editorial decision (see CED, page xv) and contrasts, for example, with the treatment of *deck* and *decoy*. These are nearby words that are treated in the order *n.* and then *vb.*

From the concordances we can glean the following distribution, confining the decision to *vb.* and *n.*

vb.	n.	TOTAL
136	109	245

Fig. 1

Verbal use predominates. Let us now break down the figures for each separate form:

		verb	noun
decline		14	108
declined		76	0
declining		38	0
declines		8	1
TOTAL	245	136	109

Fig. 2

The uninflected form, which appears as headword, does not follow the pattern of the others, but overwhelmingly is used as a noun.

We must also note that the classification of *declining* as verbal is a misleading convention; 26 of its occurrences are noun modifiers, closest in syntax to the word class *adjective*. If this point is reflected in the word-class analysis the picture changes:

		verbal	nominal	adjectival
decline		14	108	0
declined		76	0	0
declining		12	0	26
declines		8	1	0
TOTAL	245	110	109	26

Fig. 3

The different proportions of verb and noun evaporate.

At this point, before we consider the division into senses, we can associate the form *decline* with nominal usage, *declining* with adjectival usage and *declines*, *declined*, with verbal usage. The proportions of total usage of each form are given in Fig. 4.

	verbal	nominal	adjectival	Total
decline.	0.12	0.88		1.00
declined	1.00			1.00
declining	0.33		0.67	1.00
declines	0.89	0.11		1.00
TOTAL	0.46	0.44	0.10	1.00

Fig. 4

de+cline (dɪˈklaɪn) *vb.* **1.** to refuse to do or accept (something), esp. politely. **2.** (*intr.*) to grow smaller; diminish: *demand has declined over the years.* **3.** to slope or cause to slope downwards. **4.** (*intr.*) to deteriorate gradually, as in quality, health, or character. **5.** *Grammar,* to state or list the inflections of (a noun, adjective, or pronoun), or (of a noun, adjective, or pronoun) to be inflected for number, case, or gender. Compare **conjugate** (sense 1). ∼*n.* **6.** gradual deterioration or loss. **7.** a movement downward or towards something smaller; diminution. **8.** a downward slope; declivity. **9.** *Archaic.* any slowly progressive disease, such as tuberculosis. [C14: from Old French *decliner* to inflect, turn away, sink, from Latin *dēclināre* to bend away, inflect grammatically] —**de+ˈclin+a·ble** *adj.*—**de+ˈclin+er** *n.*

Fig. 5: *CED entry for* **decline**

Of the five verbal senses in CED, nos. 3 (slope gradually) and 5. (Grammar) can be discarded, because they do not occur [But for sense 3 consider App. B, 11—ed.]. Senses 2 and 4 are very hard to separate, and only sense 1 stands out. We shall continue with some observations on sense 1; note that there is no corresponding nominal sense.

Although there are only 14 instances of the base form used as a verb, they are worth looking at individually because the base form:

(a) is in the present tense, and so can refer to the moment of speaking;
(b) can take all pronouns as subject except *he, she, it*;
(c) is the imperative form.

Eight of the fourteen instances are of sense 1. Of these, one illustrates clearly what Austin called a *performative* use. The occurrence of the sentence actually performs the act named by the verb. In saying "I decline . . ." you decline:

"I decline to fuse with Tammy Hall . . ."

Many English verbs, by their meaning, could have performative uses, but by no means all are used as such; *insult* is an example. Others are not used directly, but only through modal verbs, etc. For example "I'll have to charge you £3" could be performative, whereas "I charge £3 for this job" is a report, not the verbal presentation of a bill.

There appear to be no such restraints on *decline*, though further instances would be helpful.

The distribution of sense 1 over all the forms of *decline* as verb is as follows:

	Sense 1	Total occurrences as verb	Total occurrences
decline	8	14	122
declined	36	76	76
declining	3	12	38
declines	1	8	9
TOTALS	48	110	245

Fig. 6

From this it is clear that only the form *declined* supports sense 1. We shall look further into the pattern of *declined*.

Sense 1 is distinguishable from the others on syntactic grounds. The *-ed* form has several syntactic roles, and in the pattern of *declined* we only need to pursue two of these:

(a) The simple past tense—50 instances;
(b) Following *have* etc. to make a perfect verb tense—23 instances.

There are two instances of the word functioning as a non-finite verb in a clause [App. A, 28, App. B, 8—ed.], one of them in a title [App. B, 8—ed.]; one instance of *declined* as a noun-modifier [App. B, 17—ed.], and nothing else. Specifically, there are two important roles which are not instanced at all:

(c) following *be* etc. to make the passive;
(d) clause complement [as in *The request seemed declined.*—ed.].

Sense 1 is almost confined to occurrence as the simple past tense; there are only 3 cases where it is preceded by an auxiliary, whereas half of the remaining occurrences are of that type.

In clause structure, Sense 1 can occur in transitive structures—hence one might have expected one or two passives. Of the 36 instances only 12 are in transitive structures (including clauses acting as objects). They are listed and numbered in Appendix A. 15 are followed by an infinitive clause, e.g. *to do so* (No. 24), which expresses what was declined, and count almost as the equivalent of transitivity in information terms. This leaves 9 intransitives, which merit a further glance.

The limitations of this particular concordance format become apparent at this point, whereas in the basic analysis of meaning they have rarely been a frustration. But now we are concerned with textual reference, and may need a longer citation to confirm a hypothesis.

The hypothesis is that whatever is reported as having been declined has already been named, mentioned, or indicated with sufficient clarity, so that the reader, arriving at the word *declined*, need be in no doubt about what would be a suitable object or infinitive clause. In No. 6 the pronoun *one* refers back to a relevant noun phrase, and in 12 and 18 there are prior clauses which mention what is declined (12 *if he would not dance for us*, 18 *wished to see me urgently*). In No. 19 there is the subject *it* of the next clause which continues a chain of cohesion.

In the other four cases we just have to guess at what was declined, but that indeterminacy is not a serious flaw. The crucial point is to reach agreement that in each instance there is evidence that what is declined will be found earlier in the text.

If I can assume such agreement, then all the instances of the first meaning are "text-transitive". Whatever is declined is expressed in the text in one way or another. This improves on the classic indecision of dictionaries about transitivity, enshrined in the meaningless message *v.t.+i*, and discreetly suppressed to *vb.* in CED.

CED leaves us with two verbal senses which echo nominal ones [Cf Atkins, this volume, "Grammatical classification . . .", pp. 17–19—ed.]:

2. to grow smaller; diminish
   7. a movement downward or towards something smaller; diminution
4. to deteriorate gradually, as in quality, health, or character
   6. gradual deterioration or loss.

Sense 7 expresses the difficulty of separating these senses:

(a) they are rather close together, concerning reductions in quantity and quality. In CED sense 2 quotes *diminish* whose own entry in turn quotes *depreciate*;
(b) those instances which are pretty clearly of sense 2/7 nevertheless carry a strong shading of sense 4/6.

The pattern is a small-scale example of the indeterminancy of categorization which is brought out in Stock (1984). My tentative assignments are set out in Fig. 7, which excludes the 48 instances of Sense 1, but the overwhelming impression is that categorization here is an artificial exercise. Appendix B contains all the instances of *declined* except for those which are clearly sense 1.

	mainly sense 2/7	medial or doubtful	mainly sense 4/6	Total
NOUN USES	21	18	70	109
decline	20	18	70	108
declines	1			1
VERB USES	36	14	12	62
decline	3	1	2	6
declined	24	9	7	40
declines	3	3	1	7
declining	6	1	2	9
ADJECTIVE USES (declining)	15	4	7	26
TOTAL	72	36	89	197

Fig. 7

There is a small amount of structural evidence to distinguish these senses in the case of *decline* (noun). It tends towards the "deterioration" sense when there is no qualifying phrase in the noun group, and where the qualifier is an *of*-phrase. The "deterioration" sense is likely when there is a possessive modifier, and in the phrase *in decline*. On the other hand, a qualifier which is an *in*-phrase usually signals the sense of size reduction.

These structural points are not matched by anything in the verbal uses, where all the gradations between the two senses can be found. In one example, where they are yoked together, there is no suggestion of a pun on the verb meaning.

> The RCP declined in spirit and in numbers (App. B, 33)

Collocational evidence often supports the sense of reduction in size with numerals, *per*, *average*; *population*, *economic*, *profitability*; *gradual*, *sharp*, *slowly*. The sense of deterioration is supported by, for example, *sad*, *quality*, *Britain*, *commitment*, *suffered*. Strangly, perhaps, the word *rapid* is associated with this sense.

The result of this study is that there are no sharp boundaries within a fairly broad sense-area. Most examples are a blend of the two main senses, and many are not at all clear on the constitution of the blend.

From this brief example, we can make suggestions for how *decline* should be handled in a dictionary. If we assume that the primary categorization should be by sense, then there is only one major distinction in sense, between the "refuse" sense and the "reduce" one. The slight indications of an earlier sense of "slope" might be mentioned or ignored according to the policy of the dictionary.

With respect to the "reduce" continuum it would be important to note that on the whole, nominal usage tends towards "deteriorate" while verbal and adjectival use shows the opposite inclination. The form *decline* is heavily nominal, *declining* adjectival, *declined* verbal. Instances which carry little or no trace of the "deteriorate" sense are of a slightly technical nature—economic journalism and the like.

The other main sense, of "refuse", is verbal, associated particularly with *declined*. Syntactically it is text-transitive, and pragmatically it is performative.

The general conclusion is that much more precision can be gained in lexicography by studying instances, even in the earliest stages, where we are doing little more than gathering instances together. There is at present hardly any relevant theory to guide us, and further advances can be expected with the formulation of theoretical positions—on collocational structure, on the constitution of a phrase, on the interaction between structure and sense. This should be paralleled by technical developments in our ability to handle and analyse the instances. The room for development in lexicography is enormous.

References

Harris, A., *Wordlist Design*, M.A. thesis, University of Birmingham (forthcoming).
Hofland, K. & Johannson, S., *Word Frequencies in British and American English*, Bergen, 1982.
Phillips, M. *Lexical Macrostructure in Science Text*, Ph.D. thesis, University of Birmingham, 1983.

Renouf, A., *Corpus Linguistics. Recent advances in the use of computer corpora in English Language Research*, Rodopi, 1984.

Roe, P., *The Notion of Difficulty in Scientific Text*, Ph.D. thesis, University of Birmingham, 1977.

Sinclair, J. M., *Naturalness in Language*, University of Nijmegen, 1984.

Stock, P., "Polysemy", in *Lexicographica series Maior: LEXeter '83 Proceedings*, ed. R.R.K. Hartmann, Niemayer: Tübingen, 1984.

Yang, H.-Z., "JDEST Computer Corpus of Texts of English for Science and Technology", in *ICAME News*, Bergen, forthcoming.

APPENDIX A   *Declined* in Sense 1

1.	d the Governor in respect to Hearst.' When Hearst	declined,	Al Smith continued with his meeting, den
2.	ndidate for East Surrey. But on each occasion, he	declined.	He was a zeaous Cobdenite freetrader wh
3.	ng ⟨P 208⟩ was to say: "Have some eland", which I	declined.	It was a dish of minced eland, the big b
4.	MSELF STRONGLY IN FAVOUR OF FREE SPEECH. BUT HE	DECLINED	TO RE-PUDIATE CONTROVERSIAL TACTICS OF
5.	ived at the television studio perfectly sober and	declined	all refreshments thereafter, but absurd,
6.	ket of Bastos, offered one to the Englishman, who	declined,	and lit one for himself. "That is not so
7.	article on "Male chauvinism, British style." She	declined,	and they didn't ask again. She found she
8.	ounced before telling him about it, he gracefully	declined,	and shortly afterwards Sir Robert Bignold
9.	ipal Ownership League on 4 October 1905, modestly	declined,	and then accepted five days later as a p.
10.	ph was in his own performance. The battles he had	declined	else-where, he won in the face below his
11.	g it all at Sujhir's disposal. ⟨P 214⟩ but Sudhir	declined	everything, even to sit down, so they par
12.	n we asked Gopal if he would not dance for us, he	declined	firmly but said his Gura would perform in
13.	last Friday "the darkest [night] of my life"—and	declined	further comment. The last word belonged t
14.	chool in the pony trap for the Easter Egg Hunt. I	declined	her offer. She urged that I should suppor
15.	us: he had asked an enormous fee, we regretfully	declined	his services. There was an awkward interv
16.	ython era was invited to appear in this film but	declined	it—because I think Brooks has actually
17.	tled down his throat. He offered me the bottle. I	declined	it, as he knew I would. I had rather kiss
18.	ady wished to see me urgently. I made excuses and	declined	politely but two minutes later my bedroom
19.	trip on this railway from Greenwich to London. He	declined	saying it was a "needless risk to run". A
20.	t a special part was being written in for him. He	declined	the offer and returned to his garret. I
21.	an think of no way of stopping him, though he has	declined	the invitation to address Boon as "Charle
22.	ement and to avoid the fellow-traveller's tag. He	declined	to speak at the Labour Party rally in Hyd
23.	ng them. (He was very impatient with students who	declined	to copy.) He had trouble with upright sha
24.	nd grew their hair but a few of the more ruthless	declined	to do so, they had clearly not addressed
25.	ned the invasion in the most forthright terms but	declined	to take any action whatever, however dipl
26.	e allowed to address the Court, but the Governors	declined	to give an immediate answer to the studen
27.	at at short notice." The Vice-Chancellor's Office	declined	to comment.—Rummidge Morning Post RIOT
28.	ake it worse!' [w?—Ed.]e frequently had requests, always	declined,	to keep things out of the paper. Several
29.	the cause of death was not made public, Mr Santos	declined	to comment. Brody looked up from the pap
30.	; except one, ex-President Grover Cleveland, who	declined	to allow his sorrow for those who died to
31.	ave other qualities," said Oliver Barrett III but	declined	to elaborate. (I doubt if he could have.)
32.	was now to enter—the lad gravely and resolutely	declined	to carry the thing a step further. And at
33.	ion. I think it very significant that the UDA had	declined	to attend this mass rally in the past, a
34.	isitor. What if I had turned the handle, the door	declined	to open and someone had observed my actio
35.	that the four-man crew included one Briton, but	declined	to identify him. The others were said by
36.	himself strongly in favour of free speech. But he	declined	to repudiate controversial tactics of peo

APPENDIX B Declined—Remainder of concordance

1.	its contribution to national student politics has	declined,	Attempts to launch an Alternative left o
2.	ts, did they not, Clay Jones? Jones: They rapidly	declined,	Bill Sowerbutts. Often, they would disa
3.	spiral could get worse, as the level of activity	declined,	But, on Keynesian arguments, this could
4.	ntries—real ⟨P 67⟩ disposable spending power has	declined,	But for how long will the trade unions a
5.	licy towards the west, her active involvement has	declined,	But in the visits of British Maoists to p
6.	know that the sort of lot of people generally has	declined,	((C)) Oh, it has. There are figures to p
7.	In 1966. But since 1971 the WPPE's influence has	declined,	Frequent changes of address, the failure
8.	ian Defence, the Muzio Gambit, the Queen's Gambit	declined,	Most of them are not only learned for t
9.	nt, and in that one Month, the crime rate sharply	declined,	Our Political Opponents and other Bodies
10.	attlefield, as distinct from the rear areas, soon	declined,	Refugees were posing an acute and growin
11.	izon became level and blue and clipped as the sun	declined,	That was another time of comparative coo
12.	t that our industrial performance has relatively	declined,	against that of other countries. If
13.	made her an importer. The value of her currency	declined,	along with the purchasing power of her
14.	he had not read the report. Slowly, the industry	declined,	and its members took up other activities
15.	5, pressure in the United States since prices have	declined,	and costs have gone up," explained a GE
16.	he Second World War, modernist Fine Art in France	declined,	and fell; in Britain it barely survived
17.	es also miners or railway workers, for so long in	declined,	and troubled industries. Many varied moti
18.	, psychology and so on, and they've certainly not	declined,	as a whole. Our numbers of applications e
19.	workers in the total working population actually	declined,	between 1911 and 1941'. Class divisions w
20.	p's own interest in the physical side of marriage	declined,	but he persuaded himself that this was o
21.	from 18 to 9 percent in the market; Lucky Strike	declined,	even more sharply, from 14 to 6 per cent.
22.	d so far, and had been told so often that she had	declined,	even further, that she eagerly adopted th
23.	number of paddy holdings, and their average size	declined,	from four-fifths to half an acre. Many
24.	he share of the rural areas in total population	declined,	from an average of 84 percent in 1950 to
25.	in terms of seats: the number of Congress Members	declined,	from 371 to 361; the CPI stayed steady at
26.	ain's share of world shipbuilding had as a result	declined,	from 50% in 1914 to under 10% in 1964. In
27.	rship has stagnated and its electoral performance	declined,	further, a whole range of new organisatio
28.	in March (and a revision discovered they had not	declined,	in February after all). Wage settlement
29.	farms and farm families in New England has not	declined,	in 1970, and the average age of farmers
30.	instead. Surprisingly, however, this tendency has	declined,	in the mid-1970s, and savings have remain
31.	per head of population has in some cases actually	declined,	in the last ten years among the developin
32.	oded messages received by a ordinary person has	declined,	in favour of coded messages. We may guess
33.	t, let alone against a Labour government. The RCP	declined,	in spirit and in numbers and in 1949 diss
34.	—is this still the case, or have social sciences	declined,	in undergraduate popularity? Well, first
35.	t the British Aircraft Industry is defunct; it's	declined,	of course: the Americans are the leaders
36.	ited range fires. But the number of prairie fires	declined,	sharply with the white man's arrival. As
37.	ehaves in imagination. It may be that Britain had	declined,	so far, and had been told so often that s
38.	nization. With many thousands in jail, membership	declined,	to half a million by late 1936, and the a
39.	, it is true that the authority of parliament has	declined,	with the growth of the great producer in
40.	, The average age of dwellings has steadily	declined,	writes E. F. Carter of the Stanford Res

III. APPLICATIONS OF AND ALTERNATIVES TO DICTIONARIES

THE LEARNER AS LEXICOGRAPHER: USING DICTIONARIES IN SECOND LANGUAGE LEARNING

RICHARD ROSSNER

The Bell School, Cambridge

Dr Johnson is known to have found dictionary-making "dull work" although, according to Boswell, he only spent three years on his *Dictionary, with a Grammar and History of the English Language* (less than a tenth of the time devoted by James Murray to the *Oxford English Dictionary*). However, I find his comment in the preface of the fourth edition more insightful: "He that undertakes to compile a Dictionary, undertakes that which, if it comprehends the full extent of his design, he knows himself unable to perform."* This feeling is echoed in more dramatic terms by Murray himself in a letter to his son Aelfric: "And many a time . . . when absolutely at the end of my own resources in dealing with entangled and difficult words . . . I have shut the door, and thrown myself on the floor absolutely on God's help . . . and I believe I have never asked in vain. There are many articles in the Dictionary which could never have been done by me without this earnest and agonized appeal to higher wisdom to inspire me with fresh effort." (Murray, 1977: 308–9).

The Plight of the Lexicographer

There is no question that the task of the lexicographer is unenviable, the more so because a dictionary, when all is said and done, is such a peculiarly limited instrument. The years that lexicographers sweat away in distilling from the work of their predecessors and a sea of ultimately random citations definitions for the lexical items they have decided to include seem a curious waste if one accepts (as I believe one must) a view of language as inextricably bound up with "context of situation" (in Firth's words), and as therefore a quicksilver, highly dynamic and unpredictable artefact. True, the ortho-

---

* Superscript numbers are to Notes at end of article.

graphic, grammatical, etymological and phonological information (when provided) is both useful and interesting if accurate and detailed enough to be valid wherever the language in question is commonly spoken. On the other hand, there is no denying that the time-honoured recourse of arranging entries alphabetically has serious disadvantages for many users who are interested in the differences in meaning among related words. At present such users have to buy a second book and will presumably continue to be ill-served in this way until micro-computers come with large enough memories (and small enough price tags) to compete with multi-book (and costly-to-update) systems of reference.

Even allowing for future developments, all that the immense efforts of the lexicographers can offer the user is a selection of definitions frozen in time and incapable of admitting the vast range of uses and meanings (or, in Widdowson's terms, "values"[2]) that are likely to attach themselves to lexical items in the vast range of discourse types, situations and contexts in which they will occur. How can dictionaries and their makers ever take full account of the fact that:

> Words strain,
> Crack and sometimes break, under the burden,
> Under the tension, slip, slide, perish,
> Decay with imprecision, will not stay in place,
> Will not stay still. (T. S. Eliot, "Burnt Norton")?

Yet, it so often seems, it is on this quality of words that human relations, literature, the success or failure of politicians, the fate of the world, no less, appears to depend.

The Plight of the Second-language Learner

If the task of lexicographers is hard, the task of second-language learners is harder still when it comes to evolving a lexicon that is both optimally useful and reliable. Interlanguage theory seems to cast the learner in the role of amateur lexicographer: subconsciously or consciously, learners form hypotheses about how, in general, the second language works and what, specifically, given lexical items in the second language mean. But in the formation, and confirmation or disconfirmation of these "hypotheses", learners must live by their wits. The data available for analysis do not come in neat bundles of citations painstakingly gathered by aficionados who have the background fully to interpret the discourse from which their selected citations are derived (though some teachers try to do a bit of this for their learners, at least in the early stages). No, normally learners are offered a bewildering hotchpotch of comprehensible and less comprehensible "input" (cf. Krashen, 1981) in which items may occur fairly frequently, only occasionally or hardly ever. From this they try to distil sufficient sense to assign a provisional definition for items previously unknown to them, necessarily using their mother tongue as a framework. While all this is going on, it must be remembered, learners, unlike lexicographers, will probably not use an alphabetic or other guiding system of progressing from one item to another for experience in seeking means of confirming their suppositions or dealing with homonymy and polysemy. On the other hand, while learners usually have little control over the language "data" they are exposed to, they will, because they are human, be seeking to make those conceptual and semantic links usually only touched on in thesauruses, as well as to collect (subconsciously) information about each item like that normally found in alphabetical dictionaries. Last but not least, the tools and systems used for actually recording, if the need is felt, and recalling this lexicographic information are likely to be improvised and experimental or untried.

Of course, learners also have great advantages over lexicographers in their work: first, they are probably not working to a deadline (however elastic) or aiming at a given number of entries. Also, their lexicon can remain in rough-and-ready form, indeed must do so if further development and progress along the interlanguage continuum is to be possible. There is no need to polish and refine it so that others can use it. And perhaps the greatest advantage: the entries will ultimately be a matter of personal choice; what individual learners do not like or need, or simply cannot cope with, they can usually leave out or postpone until a later "edition". Indeed, it is this personal investment and selection in the task that makes the job of learning a second language feasible.

The Qualities of the Learner's Lexicon

In spite of learners' inadequate preparation for the task, and in spite of the chaotic way they are obliged to go about it, we can, I think, be confident that the learner's home-made and often totally unrecorded lexicon is superior to the average dictionary in several ways. First, it does not have that spurious air of authority and finality but remains fluid, open to change and correction at any moment (so long as the learner is ready for it). Second, it contains no information that is redundant or uninteresting to the user: there is no waste. Third, it combines look-up and thesaurus capabilities effortlessly. Of course, it is also inferior to the printed dictionary in several ways: much more of the information that the user actually needs (sometimes desperately) is missing because the "page" in question hasn't been finished or is "illegible"; in particular, there may be a definition or two against an entry but crucial grammatical, orthographic or phonological information may be incomplete or erroneous. It is impermanent, sometimes ephemeral, so that entries are "lost" or too faintly "printed." And then, because of the way citations are gathered and other information about items collected, the number of errors may be huge.

I need not take this comparison any further, for all of us, whether second-language learners or not, are also lexicographers in this limited but astonishingly productive and dynamic sense; and we all know intuitively how superior our own "entries" are when it comes to coping with connotation and the malleable, perishable qualities of lexical items that Eliot speaks of. First language users know, even if second-language learners are obliged to forget it temporarily, that what dictionary-makers seem to chisel in stone, we can mould like plasticine.

The Teacher as Assistant Editor

Second-language learners who have access to teachers may expect useful assistance when it comes to building up the lexical repertoire (cf Anthony 1975) they need in order to become competent communicators in the language. Especially when learning is taking place in the mother-tongue environment, the teacher can be extremely useful in providing comprehensible input from which "citations" or other evidence can be gathered. Teachers can also assist learners in forming hypotheses or altering them, in completing information that may be partly lacking and in trying to "cover" some of the lexical gaps. More importantly, teachers can provide learners with opportunities for using their lexicons both pragmatically in a restricted way, and creatively in an unrestricted way, and in the light of what happens try to improve the accuracy and reliability of the provisional information so far entered. Then there is a useful role for teachers in actually assisting learners in evolving frameworks for recording information they wish to record systematically: teachers can be design consultants. But it has to be remembered that language learning is essentially a research task which has to be done by the learner. It is learners themselves who have to analyse data and come to conclusions about what the results mean; it is the learners themselves who must take the risks and gather the feedback, though there is much room for moral support and guidance.

The Learner and Vocabulary: Ways of Using the Dictionary

Rigid procedures in language learning have long since ceased to be convincing, because of either psycholinguistic or humanitarian reservations. But there is a range of encounters and experiments with vocabulary that are known to be useful to learners of different kinds at different times. This is not to imply that the possibilities mentioned below are the only worthwhile ones or that all learners find them useful. Individualization is increasingly seen as crucial in language learning, and in no aspect of it more than in the development of a repertoire of vocabulary, which by its nature must be highly individual.

The order below is of no particular significance.

1. Whether the first encounter with "new" lexical items is carefully stage-managed in a classroom or in self-study materials, or happens while walking down a street in a "target-language environment", it is here that the bilingual dictionary comes into its own: bafflement is of little use to the learner, who is likely to forget any item that does not impinge further on his or her consciousness than baffling does. The small pocket bilingual dictionary will offer little more than a rough translation, but, in Michael Swan's words, it gives the learner a mother-tongue peg to hang the new item on.[3] The same goes for encounters in the classroom: the backlash that followed the demise of grammar-translation techniques in the sixties often meant active censure of the (natural) pursuit of mother-tongue equivalents. Bilingual dictionaries were banned and learners who exchanged hypotheses about mother-tongue equiva-

lents sotto voce were reprimanded. Instead we conducted an elaborate guessing game, not unlike the famous party games on the "charades" theme and complete with mime, circumlocutions and word-association tests. More recently we have seen a happy (in my view) swing back to permissiveness; learners, even in the confusingly multilingual classrooms of Britain and the U.S., no longer have to hide their bilingual dictionaries or resist the temptation of mother-tongue impurity of thought.

Of course, there are many dangers in bilingual dictionaries, particularly the tiny ones designed to be consulted furtively and secreted about the person: often only one-word equivalents are possible due to column width, and only one or two "frequent" meanings are offered. What if there are cultural barriers that make one-word equivalence impossible (false equivalents like Fr. *château*—Eng. *castle* spring to mind)? Or what if the meaning dealt with in the dictionary offers no clue as to the meaning which the item has in the context of encounter? But this does not rule such dictionaries out for the learner at the basic level. Nor does it rule out the much more elaborate bilingual dictionary for learners at the advanced level who find translation a useful awareness-raising and accuracy-promoting activity. For here the whole point of the dictionary is that very often it can do little more than provide a clue, a starting point for the process of finding the optimum equivalent via the complex semantic networks in which words in both languages are stored, according to the way the meanings of items in the discourse being translated "intersect" (Anthony, 1975).

2. Some learners seem to find it profitable physically to construct a lexicon in note form or on cards. Adrian Underhill and Roger Gower have suggested[3] actually mapping out grids in which information can be collected about meaning, grammatical constraints, pronunciation, etc., and in which examples collected from various sources can be gathered. This can also be done communally on a wall display.[4] A card-index system will allow for accretion of the lexicon in a more convenient alphabetical or semantic way. In all cases, learners (and the teacher) will need to have a variety of dictionaries and other reference books available for consultation either during or between lessons. Although at basic and intermediate stages ALD[5] or LDOCE,[5] plus the Longman *Lexicon* (McArthur, 1982), and ODCIE[5] will probably be sufficient for learners of English, at more advanced levels, larger, more informative dictionaries and *Roget's Thesaurus* will need to be added.

Procedures vary: some teachers and learners prefer to set aside time in class specifically for vocabulary work based on reading or listening texts. Learners are assigned words or groups of words in a semantic set and are asked to "research" them outside class time using the reference books and collecting what other examples they can. The allotted class-time is then taken up with reporting back. Others prefer to deal only with words that learners select as "interesting" or "useful" and to make the person who "nominates" the item responsible for finding out more about it. Either way, teacher guidance and the proper use of dictionaries will be crucial. It has to be remembered that many learners come to the second language with little or no experience of using dictionaries in their mother tongue; it may therefore be necessary to offer a short course in dictionary-using skills, doing activities such as those suggested for learners of English in Underhill's useful *Use Your Dictionary*. This is that much more important where there are differences of script resulting in unfamiliarity with alphabet order.

3. At a more individual level, especially when learning is taking place in a target-language environment, learners can be encouraged to note down interesting/useful items they find in the language they are exposed to, preferably complete with some context (e.g. a whole sentence) and some notes on the situation (speaker/writer, place, purpose, etc.). This can then be followed up with dictionary work and comparisons with other items. Such personal research, which can be stimulated by setting aside time for learners to report back on their "most interesting words of the week", is particularly useful when items are involved that learners have already encountered previously, in other words if a new use or grammatical constraint or an addition to the "spectrum of meaning" (Anthony 1975) is dealt with. Here interest and awareness can be stimulated by some introductory work in the mother tongue where this is possible, for one of the advantages of this type of text analysis is that it can throw new light not only on the second language but on language in general.

4. In recent articles, Harvey (1983) and Stieglitz (1983) have shown how even at basic and intermediate levels procedures borrowed from "lexical decomposition" can be adapted to get learners to explore lexical sets. At the advanced level, Rudzka *et al.* (1981, 1985) have provided a whole bookful of materials aimed at sensitizing advanced learners to both the componential and the collocational common ground between items in sets. Learners seem to enjoy such work however controversial it may seem to be borrowing from linguistics in this way. Certainly, there seems little harm in getting learners on their own or in groups to define and explore sets of words that are semantically related. Here works like the Longman *Lexicon* will prove useful, but learners will also need to consult a range of other dictionaries. One approach to this is to set lexical tasks as introductions to other activities such as discussion of a topic, role-play or written composition. The topic in each case is likely to suggest sematic areas, which learners can offer to develop in a descriptive way before the more "communicative" activity. The aim, then, would *not* be for learners to attempt to use those items thrown up by the descriptive work in their discussion, role-play, etc. Rather, the hope would be that the descriptive task would serve as a reminder or as a means of increasing awareness of the possibilities. Alternatively, learners may prefer to consider words which were used and those which might have been used, and how they relate to one another, *after* a communicative activity (e.g. listening to tape recordings of it, and listing and researching words that were used and words which weren't in a given topic area).

5. As early as possible, learners need to be made aware of how the same lexical item can fulfil very different functions in different circumstances, and of how lexical items vary in the degree of markedness or emotive overtone they carry. Here exercises such as that offered on p. 129 of Barr *et al.* (1981), in which learners are asked to assign positive, negative or neutral "connotation" to

lexical items as used in a text, can be useful, as can text-analysis exercises in which learners are asked to explain why speakers/writers use a given item rather than others that are similar in meaning. This will become more important still in courses where learners are working with poems and other literary texts in which association, connotation and allusion as well as the phonological and grammatical qualities of items are thrown into relief. Here research into regular collocations and co-occurence, for example, by reference to dictionaries that list citations, may help learners to see what kind of effect the writer is trying to achieve, and to judge in their own terms how successful it is.

6. Where lexis shades off into grammar, dictionaries retain their usefulness. Dictionaries for learners of English such as ALD and LDOCE, for example, include lists of sentence patterns and cross references to them so that learners can see what patterns a given item works in and which it is not normally used in. An apparently straightforward exercise, such as finding out which of a list of verbs of motion that are normally used intransitively can also be used in transitive sentence patterns, can be done with a good learners' dictionary. Learners can then be asked to give examples with those verbs that have transitive uses (almost all verbs of motion in English). With advanced students, similar systematic work can be done in the area of affixes (see Bolinger's paper and Underhill's section 4 in this volume). The constraints on combinations of roots and affixes are complex, but the morphology of lexical items is particularly generative, especially in English, and especially from the learner's point of view. What is more, unlike the total lexicon of the language, the affixes of a language like English seem to constitute a finite set (cf. Quirk *et al.*, 1972: 981–1008). Learners can be asked to consider a suffix or pair of suffixes like Bolinger's *-less* and *-ful* and to research their range of usefulness with noun roots. Having pooled their various repertoires of words in *-less* and *-ful*, they could hypothesize other candidates for these suffixes, confirm or disconfirm them using the dictionary, search speculatively for (and possibly bet on!) others, and try to work out where and how the two groups differ, how *hopeful* and *spoonful* compare, how *worthless* and *priceless* differ, and so on. An experiment I have yet to try is to get learners at the advanced level to devise and write vocabulary exercises of this kind for each other (a single class could generate a lot of useful exercises!).

Conclusion

The work of lexicographers, then, is not just similar to that of second-language learners in some ways; the fruits of it are very useful in language learning. But the usefulness of dictionaries to language learners must not be overestimated either. Whether learners use dictionaries for some of the purposes I have outlined or in other ways I have not (such as learning pages of dictionaries by heart, which may not be as silly as it sounds from some learners' points of view), what learners gain from the dictionary will be cold and static. It will be like studying roadsigns in a driving manual, not like interpreting roadsigns when behind the wheel or handlebars. For dictionaries are only an attempt to abstract rules and boundaries from instances of use and intuition, but in the end, indeed throughout, it is creative use, not the rules that seem to govern it, that concerns learners. They have more rights and fewer duties than lexicographers, and shouldn't forget it.

Notes

1. See Boswell's *Life of Johnson*, Macmillan 1898, p 98.
2. In *Teaching Language as Communication* (OUP 1978, p 10–12), Widdowson makes the distinction between "signification", propositional meaning that can be attributed to language outside communicative contexts, and "value", the meaning "sentences and parts of sentences assume when they are put to use for communicative purposes". Thus, according to this definition, dictionaries can only cope with "signification", though part of the lexicographer's task will involve abstracting "signification" from "values" assumed by lexical items in the various citations referred to.
3. In February 1983, at an ARELS conference on the teaching of vocabulary in Eastbourne, I was involved in a group discussion with Michael Swan, Roger Gower, Adrian Underhill and Steve Walters, whose ideas and experience I draw on freely here. [Cf. Underhill, this volume, p. 113, top—Ed.]
4. I have seen this done in Diana Fried-Booth's classes at the Bell School of Languages, Bath.
5. ALD: *Oxford Advanced Learner's Dictionary of English*
   LDOCE: *Longman Dictionary of Contemporary English*
   ODCIE: *Oxford Dictionary of Current Idiomatic English* Vols 1 and 2.

References

Anthony, E. M. (1975) *Towards a Theory of Lexical Meaning*, Singapore: RELC.

Barr, P., J. Clegg and C. Wallace (1981) *Advanced Reading Skills*, London: Longman.

Harvey, P. (1983) "Vocabulary learning: the use of grids". *ELT Journal* 37.3: 243–6.

Krashen, S. (1981) *Second Language Acquisition and Second Language Learning*, Oxford: Pergamon Press.

McArthur, T. (1981) *Longman Lexicon of Contemporary English*, London: Longman.

Murray, K. M. E. (1977) *Caught in the Web of Words*, New Haven, Conn. & London: Yale University Press.

Quirk, R. *et al.* (1972) *A Grammar of Contemporary English*, London: Longman.

Lloyd, S. (ed.) (1982) *Roget's Thesaurus* (6th edition), London: Longman.

Rudzka, B. *et al.* (1981) *The Words you Need*, London & Basingstoke: Macmillan.

Rudzka, B. *et al.* (1985) *More Words you Need*, London & Basingstoke: Macmillan.

Stieglitz, E. (1983) "A practical approach to vocabulary reinforcement". *ELT Journal* **37.1**: 71–5.

Underhill, A. (1980) *Use your Dictionary*, Oxford: O.U.P.

WORKING WITH THE MONOLINGUAL LEARNERS' DICTIONARY

ADRIAN UNDERHILL

International House, Hastings

In this article I am going to discuss ways of using dictionaries to increase the effectiveness of students' language learning. Before doing that I shall highlight some of the problems associated with the attempt to give dictionaries a more central position in daily class activities.

The article is addressed to teachers, materials writers, syllabus designers and lexicographers, all of whom I hope will benefit from a review of the present state of play in this area and from a general disentangling of the separate strands of the problem. In all of this I am speaking as a practising EFL teacher whose primary aim is to promote effective learning both in and out of the classroom

For the sake of clarity I have made frequent use of subheadings followed by numbered notes.

To start with we can distinguish three kinds of dictionary: the monolingual learners' dictionary (abbreviated throughout this article to MLD); the bilingual or translating dictionary (TD); and the native speakers' dictionary (NSD).

Most teachers would agree that one of their main tasks is to help learners to help themselves, and one way of working towards this is to train them to be effective users of a good MLD. I have found that there are few students and few teachers who do not benefit from such training. Of all the TEFL books available, the MLD can perhaps answer a greater number of students' questions about English than any other single book. Insofar as it is the teacher's responsibility to teach students how to use the MLD effectively, deciding not to do so may be to deny students the chance of attaining some degree of independence and self-confidence in their studies. Being able to use the MLD well is not only advantageous in itself, but may help to lead students into new modes of self-study. Given the right opportunities, students quickly realize that what they find out for themselves is more likely to be assimilated than what they are told.

Within the constraints of its format the MLD specifically attempts to make available to second-language learners categories of information that are pertinent to their task, while at the same time offering that information in the very language they haven't yet mastered. Because of this and in order to make the MLD accessible to the widest possible range of learner levels the authors of such dictionaries have been obliged to consider more carefully than ever before the question: "How do we maintain clarity and economy as our hallmarks and yet remain true to the language?" The degree to which they achieve this is the subject of current debate.

From my work in the classroom I have been able to observe two distinct though interacting kinds of information which learners may obtain from the dictionary. For my own convenience I call these Specific Information and Incidental Awareness. Specific Information results from the asking of a specific question which the learner somehow addresses to the dictionary, and, if he has asked his question in the most appropriate way, then the dictionary may yield an item or items which specifically answer his question (even if one kind of answer is that the dictionary does not contain that information). Incidental Awareness is everything else that the learner may notice albeit unconsciously while looking for Specific Information. Understanding the roles of these two overlapping kinds of information-getting has allowed me to exploit more fully the learning potential of the dictionary.

However before taking this further it will be useful to summarize the specific advantages of using the MLD. I will then comment on what the TD and NSD have to offer since this will help to sharpen our perception of the role of the MLD still further.

Some Advantage of Using the MLD

(1) Users have to think in English.
(2) Meanings have to be understood in terms of other English words, promoting a more rapid expansion of passive vocabulary.
(3) Many high-frequency function words which are virtually inaccessible via a TD may be given appropriate treatment.
(4) Learners may gain insights into the precision of defining and describing meanings, and constructing example sentences, as well as learning to cope with definitions which at first seem unclear.
(5) The example sentences themselves not only exemplify typical usage but also provide an alternative access to the meaning, either to substantiate the definition or to subordinate it where the example is found to be clearer.
(6) The teacher guidance often required at elementary and intermediate levels, to help learners to disentangle the information, is time spent very usefully. This is because for that moment the teacher has given to the dictionary the job of dispensing information, to the students the job of finding it, and to himself the job of remaining watchful and available to offer help at the appropriate moment.
(7) The ability to use the MLD effectively allows students the satisfaction of exploration through the dictionary, a sense of self-sufficiency and greater confidence in their ability to solve language problems for themselves. This in turn helps students to recognize and formulate their own language problems and questions in the first instance.

Some Comments on the TD

(1) The TD promises the learner access to the unknown target language via the known mother tongue, and hence it can afford a degree of security.

(2) Therefore learners who want to use TD's can be permitted to do so until they are ready to find out for themselves that there is more to be gained from using the MLD.

(3) It is the teacher's job to provide an environment conducive to this discovery.

(4) Discovering for himself the differences between the TD and the MLD will provide the learner with useful insights into the advantages and disadvantages of each.

(5) For example he begins to find out that habitual use of the TD as a way of finding out what words mean is in fact rather a slow way of enlarging his target language vocabulary, since it limits him to viewing English through the perceptions of his mother tongue. Take for instance the word *empire*. A small Spanish TD gives simply "imperio", which is the Spanish name for the Spanish version of the same concept. The MLD however gives "a group of countries under one central authority", so the TD gives a target-language synonym while the MLD defines without repeating the headword. This is important not only because it gives the learner the opportunity to learn the English concept as opposed to the Spanish concept, in case they differ, but also because "a group of countries under one central authority" indicates the meaning as well as introducing the learner to a constellation of English content words related to each other and to the original word (group . . . countries . . . central . . . authority . . .). An added extra is a syntactic setting in which the whole thing occurs (a . . . of . . . under one . . .).

(6) Many TD's give only single-word translations, as a result of which learners are bound to make mistakes. Where the TD gives more than one meaning equivalent learners need to know the difference. Again, such information is still not available in many TD's. In any case the fact that learners make mistakes using the TD because they fail to find a translation that is acceptable in the particular context does not in itself constitute a complete condemnation of the TD. Presumably they would still make mistakes without using one. How desirable or undesirable this is depends largely on the teacher's attitude towards the role of mistakes and their corrections.

(7) Since connotations, or meaning associations are not given in most TD's, what are apparently nearest translations may in fact have quite different meaning associations in the two languages. To some extent the chances of finding suitable translations in a TD depends on how closely related the two languages are.

(8) As a result of all this it may be that the TD is more suited to comprehension rather than production-type activities.

(9) Students who are initially reliant on the TD can be encouraged to move from a position of TD supported by MLD, to MLD supported by TD.

Some Comments on the NSD

(1) Many learners have already encountered an NSD in their own language at primary and secondary school. However since the mother tongue had already been acquired the role of the NSD was largely to expand vocabulary and check spelling.

(2) Since mother-tongue vocabulary expands itself naturally without a dictionary, the NSD was hardly central to the syllabus and consequently its effective exploitation was never explicitly taught. There are no grounds therefore for assuming that learners in the foreign language class come with any useful experience in the use of the dictionary.

(3) On the contrary learners may well bring with them a negative disposition towards the dictionary because it was not seen as something that made life easier, it was peripheral, its use was not taught, and the formal and uncompromising language of the definitions may have given the NSD an air of inaccessibility and dullness. Remember for example the frustration of the "dictionary chase" resulting from the overuse of synonyms often more obscure to the user than the word they are intended to clarify. I have even come across situations where copying out passages from the dictionary has been a standard form of punishment.

The main point that comes out of this is that in our dictionary work with students we should assume nothing and start from scratch in developing in the learner a positive view of dictionary use based on the discovery of its practical benefits.

What Stands in the Way of a Fuller Exploitation of the MLD?

I think there are three crucial points in answer to this question:

(1) Many teachers do not have a clear understanding of the kinds of language awareness that the MLD can be instrumental in helping learners to develop.

(2) Based partly on this ignorance teachers may well fear that their learners will resist the MLD because they in turn don't see the point of it, nor have they previously found other kinds of dictionary strikingly helpful.

(3) Often when the teacher does decide to integrate the MLD into general class work a feeling of awkwardness is experienced as when trying to use a new instrument but using it only clumsily. It is here that the teacher needs some practical guidelines so that he is not, as so often happens, reduced to introducing the MLD in an apologetic and tentative fashion which is neither integrating nor inspiring for the learners.

The solution then is to develop in teachers and students a greater awareness of how the MLD can be exploited. This can be achieved by a combination of technique and attitude which are expressed through exercises which have a high learning yield because:

(1) They cater for different learning styles by allowing different learners to work in different ways at different times, thus always allowing learners to meet the challenge at their own level.

(2) They have the power to engage the learners' attention because learners can see themselves getting the job done, and enjoying it. Motivation thus arises from meeting the challenge of the task in hand, rather than from outside or prior sources.

Exercises, games and activities that manifest these two characteristics will be referred to as having the quality of "engaging" the learner, and this quality, or set of qualities, is essential to any activity that is to have a high learning yield.

So far we have made some observations about the characteristics of the MLD compared with the TD and the NSD; we have introduced and defined Specific Information and Incidental Awareness; and we have introduced and defined the quality of engagement of the learner in the task, which should inform both the design of class activities and the attitude of the teacher in implementing them.

We can now take a close look first at dictionary activities that can engage learners in the search for specific information and then at activities that can engage learners in the exploitation of incidentally acquired awareness.

Engaging Learners in the Search for, and Exploitation of, Specific Information in the MLD

There are four main areas of Specific Information offered by the MLD:

(1) Spelling.
(2) Word pronunciation and word stress.
(3) Grammatical information.
(4) Meanings of words and phrases.

A range of ideas for classroom activities which integrate dictionary use with other classwork is now suggested for each of these four areas in turn. These suggestions concern WHAT to do in a lesson, or lesson content, as opposed to HOW to conduct the lesson, or lesson method. Both content and method need to be right if the lesson is to be effective. However in my view it is the method, the way things are done, which ultimately determines what a learner gets from a lesson. It is the way of working which determines what a learner actually does with his learning capacities.

Discussion of method is outside the scope of this article, but in reading the following content suggestions it should be borne firmly in mind that what makes them work is the way they are done and that the most important factor governing that is the teacher's attitude towards the learners, his attitude towards the activity, and his attitude towards himself and what he is doing in the class. These are the things which help determine the degree to which learners may become engaged in their learning, and hence the learning yield of the time invested.

(1) Spelling

This section of activities requires only that the dictionary be seen as a giant spelling list. Since learners are not required to retrieve information from the entry itself, but only to locate the headword, these activities form a good basis for the introduction of dictionary work at any level.

For elementary and intermediate students, take the opportunity to:

(a) Learn the English alphabet thoroughly, forwards and backwards, including the correct pronunciation of each letter.

(b) Give brief spelling dictations to practise recognition of spoken letters. Speak each group of letters as one flow. Use this for bits of language under study and for introducing new words.

(c) Do the same having students spell out their own short sentence.

(d) Give a little practice in "alphabetization", that is putting words whose first few letters are the same into alphabetical order. The words can be taken from any page in the dictionary and offered in a different order on the board, or through a spelling dictation.

For students of all levels:

(e) Whatever spelling questions arise in class they can from now on be answered with reference to the dictionary. This necessitates making some kind of guess or hypothesis about the spelling of the word in order to locate it in the dictionary especially where the unknown letters are near the beginning of the word.

(f) Work out likely spellings of single words spoken by the teacher, and check them immediately in the dictionary.

(g) Build these uses into lessons. For example, after doing a normal dictation give the students a few minutes to check with the dictionary and correct any words they think they may have misspelt. Not only does this remove the pressure of having to remember spelling and having to be right, but it also allows learners to work on a much more subtle level where they have to ask themselves which words don't look right, and then find out for themselves whether they were right in thinking that. Not only are they working at their own level on their own criteria of what constitutes acceptable English spelling, but the teacher is actually letting them do what they can for themselves instead of doing it for them by coming in too early and "correcting their mistakes" for them.

(h) This can be applied to any student writing be it composition, homework exercise, etc. Students can be given a minute or two to question their own spelling and refer to a dictionary. Once done any remaining misspellings in their work take on a special significance since their wrongness apparently does not jar the students' criteria of acceptability.

This way of working, which allows learners to demand from themselves a much higher standard of spelling without relying on the teacher, would be impossible without the integral use of the dictionary. This approach to spelling and the dictionary also serves as a useful way of introducing the dictionary to learners since it does not require them to decode the rest of the entry, but nevertheless gets them used to the general layout of the dictionary and to thumbing through its pages.

(2) Word Pronunciation and Word Stress

The activities in this section once again do not require learners to make use of the bulk of the entry but simply to refer to the phonological information given, typically in slanted brackets, immediately following the headword. As with spelling in the previous section, we shall find that there are a set of activities that can easily permeate other class activities. The exercises are integrative, so special class time set aside for dictionary practice is not required.

The learning potential of phonetic symbols in pronunciation teaching has not on the whole been very thoroughly exploited. This often seems to be justified by vague assumptions to the effect that learners have enough to do already without the gratuitous complication of having to learn unnecessary phonetic symbols. However it is suggested here that there is no inherent difficulty in the learning of phonetic symbols themselves, but rather any difficulties lie in lack of clarity of what the symbols represent, namely the sounds themselves.

Those who do not teach the phonetic symbols along with some degree of accuracy in the production of the sounds they symbolize severely underestimate both the learners' intelligence and the many advantages of phonetic symbols. Denying learners the opportunity to become familiar with phonetic symbols is to deny them:

(a) The ability to find the pronunciation and stress of any word in the dictionary,
(b) The ability to record in their own handwriting the pronunciation and stress of new words, phrases etc.,
(c) The ability to objectify the string of sounds contained in a word and to study the sequences and clusters.

With this view of the role of phonetic symbols in mind, the following types of dictionary-linked pronunciation exercises are suggested:

(a) Learning the phonemic sounds of English as given in the front cover of the Oxford and Longman MLD's and using the symbols as visual pegs on which to hang the experience of each sound so far. 44 are listed in ALD; 54 (including triphthongs and special symbols for American English) in LDOCE.
(b) Using the key words given in the cover of the MLD as mnemonic models for the phonetic sounds. Students are by now beginning to identify their own problem sounds and the related symbols.
(c) Observing the relationships between English spellings and English sounds. Using the MLD freely in connection with many aspects of word pronunciation, especially asking students to look up and check the

pronunciation of any words they may be mispronouncing. As with spelling, it is now possible to ask learners to find out new things for themselves without relying on models or information from the teacher, although the teacher is of course watching and monitoring what the students find, and helping where necessary. Note that LDOCE appends a spelling table going from phonemic symbols to their various possible English spellings.

(d) In the same way learners can use the dictionary to check primary and secondary stress, as an integral part of a word's overall pronunciation.

(e) Stress patterns in idiomatic expressions.

(f) Although the pronunciations given in the MLD refer to isolated words, i.e. citation forms, the MLD still has a wide range of applications in the classroom study of stream-of-speech English. In the analysis and practice of connected speech from tape it is a great help to learners if they are able to use phonetic script to objectify on the board what they think they are hearing. It is also a great help if learners are familiar with the MLD since then they can check the citation-form pronunciation and see in what way the taped speaker has simplified it to yield a stream-of-speech form.

(3) Grammatical Information

While the MLD offers a complete spelling list and a fairly complete pronunciation list (ultimately perhaps a subjective view of what constitutes RP citation form), it is of course very far from complete in its offering of grammatical information. What it does offer is basically what it finds convenient to offer given its format, but there is sufficient grammatical information to make it well worth while integrating the use of the MLD into the relevant parts of the syllabus. Only through using the MLD for every possible purpose will students get to know just how useful it can be.

Retrieval of the following kinds of specific grammar information requires only the scanning of the entry for the relevant symbols or abbreviations:

(a) Word class and the different classes a word may have,

(b) Forming derivatives and changing word class,

(c) Countable and uncountable nouns,

(d) Transitive and intransitive verbs,

(e) Irregular verbs, spelling changes in regular verbs, irregular noun plurals,

(f) Comparative and superlative forms of adjectives,

(g) Correct prepositions in phrases,

(h) Additionally, the Longman and Oxford advanced MLD's have their own complementation-pattern systems (e.g. for verbs) given as coded references in the entry and elaborated in full elsewhere in the dictionary.

Once the teacher has realized it, the MLD can become the source for all of this information whenever it is required during a lesson, freeing the teacher just a little from the role of information giver.

The MLD has built into it two other sources of grammatical information:

(i) The miscellaneous grammatical information implicit in the example sentences,

(j) The information available under the entry for any grammar word. For example the entries for *can, if, will, but, a, the, be,* etc. contain a good deal of information about the possible grammatical relationships of those words, presented with the needs of foreign learners in mind.

(4) Meanings of Words and Phrases

Looking up meanings is the activity generally associated with dictionaries, but as we have seen the MLD offers many other kinds of information as a result of which there are many ways of integrating the MLD into the business of learning English.

When introducing the MLD to elementary learners it is probably advisable not to begin with looking up meanings since that in fact takes so many other things for granted. It may be better to follow some kind of introductory sequence as outlined above, that is, begin with spelling activities, move on to pronunciation and grammar applications of the MLD, and only then, when students are familiar with the basic layout and workings of the MLD, begin to explore meanings.

Here are some basic uses of the MLD for finding meanings from which exercises and games can be derived and woven into class activities:

(a) When looking up a word, always note how many separate numbered headwords ("homographs") there are for that particular spelling form before deciding which is the relevant meaning.

(b) Having located the headword, note how many definitions are given within that single entry before choosing.

(c) These two kinds of exercise are fundamental to efficient dictionary use, and one of the spin-offs from them is the growing awareness of how many words in English, especially the more frequent ones, have several meanings and a variety of usages. This is something to do with what is often loosely referred to as the "richness of English"—or indeed the richness of language.

(d) Students will often need help with understanding the definition and in the earlier stages guidance in finding the right definition in the first place. The definition needs to be written on the board and analyzed as a class activity to help students to learn to spot the key words in the definitions, to get used to the language and style of definitions, and to help learners to spot the difference between synonyms and other describing language.

(e) Example sentences need to be studied not only for what they add to the definition of meaning but also for their exemplification of likely context.

(f) The MLD is generally very good in its treatment of idioms and phrasal and prepositional verbs, and can play a useful role in helping learners to come to terms with them.

(g) The MLD can be useful as learners begin to become aware of style, in particular unmarked style as against formal, informal and slang.

(h) Wordbuilding through the addition of prefixes and suffixes, and observing the relationship between the meaning of the derivative and the meaning of the root word. [Cf. Rossner, this volume, p. 101—ed.]

(i) The MLD should be available during the comprehension phases of listening and reading exercises, where the teacher will be encouraging students to find a balance between guessing meaning from context and being precise about the meaning of key words. The MLD is also useful in written compositions, and in the planning stage of communicative activities such as role play. [Cf. Rossner, this volume, p. 100, No. 4—ed.]

Engaging Learners in the Exploitation of Incidental Awareness

Whatever the entry may say, it is certainly not all there is to be said about a word. It is just a starting point for the learner's discovery of the meanings and usages of a word. In order to build up a complete picture of the constellation of possibilities that surrounds any word, students must go beyond merely finding specific answers to specific questions about single aspects of a word. In order to develop a multi-dimensional view of a word learners need to be aware of amongst other things: form, in the sense of spelling, pronunciation and stress; grammatical implications, in the sense of word class, derivatives and syntactical possibilities; and meaning, in the sense of definition, synonym, typical usage, typical collocation, stylistic value, mother-tongue translation, etc.

MLD entries can provide starting points for most of these, and if this is done systematically, its use can hasten the process of getting to know a word and its surrounding constellation of associations. The dictionary entry is not a substitute for the learner's experience of a word in action, but it can provide some initial awarenesses for the building of that experience.

I will suggest here two basic exercise types, both of which in various elaborations I have found useful in training learners to bring together their Incidental Awarenesses in order to enhance their multi-dimensional view of what learning a word involves.

(a) Having dealt with the Specific Information for which the MLD was perhaps consulted in the first place, one can then ask students the question "what else did you notice?" In answer to this students may come up with anything, no matter how incidental it may seem. For example they might have noticed or been struck by the spelling, or the stress, or a synonym, or one of the words used in the definition, or by the example sentence, or one of the derivatives, or by some link with a mother-tongue word. Some learners might be puzzled or unsure of something, and this provides a forum in which to mention this, while others may have noticed the number of homographs or senses of the headword, or what the preceding headword was, or something on the opposite page. This is actually rather an interesting exercise because students quickly become more "aware of their Incidental Awareness" and as they do so more comes out of this "what else did you notice?" game.

I have found that time spent in this way has the additional function of allowing the memory the opportunity to find its own memory hooks on which to hang various strands of information relating to the experience of looking up the word.

(b) A more formal way of training learners to be aware of Incidental Awareness, so that it becomes perhaps specifically rather than incidentally observed information, is as follows:

From a reading or listening comprehension being done in class ask students to decide on ten or so words that they are unsure of in some way, or that they would like to know more about. Ask them to write these in a column down the left side of the board. Along the top of the board write some or all of these headings: spelling, pronunciation and stress, word class, definition, synonym, example, typical use, special notes, translation. Then ask students either singly or in pairs to choose one or two of these words and with the aid of the MLD to fill in something in each column for their chosen word. Afterwards the class can discuss the findings and perhaps add improvements. This exercise does not need to be done very often to have quite a significant impact on the learners' views of what is involved in learning a word, and it also helps to bring words to life by providing a variety of things for the memory to get hold of other than just the fleeting description of a meaning. It can also provide a format for individual student vocabulary lists.

A Few Hints on Using the MLD in Class

(a) Teachers should keep an eye open for ways of integrating the dictionary with classwork. Wherever students can get information for themselves, let them do so, making sure they have some idea of what to look up.

(b) Whenever students use the dictionary, the teacher should do so as well, in order to understand problems as they occur.

(c) Don't expect students to remember everything they look up. Rather, stress the fact that if they forget, they can always look it up again.

(d) Let students use the dictionary as much for checking what they think they already know as for learning new things.

(e) A useful way of starting a lesson, perhaps while waiting for late arrivals, is to give students one or two items to check in the dictionary. These would be items occurring in the lesson anyway, and this prior self-investment may encourage more involvement.

(f) Where possible, allow students to use their MLD's in class tests and exams.

(g) The purpose of all these activities is to breathe life into dictionary usage, so that learners end up doing it for themselves rather than doing it for the teacher. The more they use the MLD, the more uses they will find for it.

Further Reading

Underhill, A., *Use Your Dictionary*, OUP, 1980.
Whitcut, J., *Learning With LDOCE*, Longman, 1979.

Monolingual Learners' Dictionaries

Oxford Advanced Learner's Dictionary of Current English (ALD)
Oxford Student's Dictionary of Current English
Longman Dictionary of Contemporary English (LDOCE)

ALTERNATIVES TO DICTIONARIES

C. P. HILL

Department of ESOL, University of London Institute of Education

There are a number of aspects of the teaching and learning of English vocabulary for speakers of other languages that appear to require constant reconsideration. One of these is the part that reference books other than dictionaries may play.

There are two limitations on ordinary dictionaries which have been frequently discussed. The first of these is what has been termed their circularity, the fact that they use words to describe words. The classic example being something like the definition of a *dog* as a "domesticated member of the canine species which includes the fox, the wolf and the coyote", and of *canine* as "of the species which includes the dog, the fox, the wolf and the coyote". The second limitation is the lack of rich context for words. Very often words take on precise meanings by virtue of the contexts within which they are used and it is almost impossible to capture this within the limits of space permitted by even the largest dictionaries.

There have been a number of valiant efforts to overcome these limitations. The extensive use of citations which produces the ever growing volumes of the great *Oxford English Dictionary* supplements is an obvious attempt to mitigate the effects of the second. The increasing use of illustrations as for example in the *Longman Dictionary of Contemporary English* is an equally obvious attempt to overcome the first.

The logical outcome of the use of illustrations must be a picture dictionary, and the best known and most fully and consistently carried through of these is the *English Duden* which was originally published in Germany in 1937, revised and updated in 1958 and published in England in 1959. The *Duden* consists of 368 pages of labelled pictures and diagrams covering some 25,000 words. The illustrations show the relation of part to whole, or in some cases the membership of a genus or species. For example, page 185 shows the various parts which go to make up a motor car, while page 348 illustrates—in colour—some of the commoner Lepidoptera: butterflies and moths. Thus there is considerable structuring of the vocabulary in conceptual and semantic field terms. The topics covered are very numerous, giving a sense of comprehensiveness as they cover atoms and zoos by way of industry, sport, travel and recreation. Access to this wealth of illustration is by way of a very full and accurate index; thus the book may be used either from term to context or from context to term. So if a term like *butterfly-valve* is looked up it will be found to appear in illustration number 183 and will be labelled 61. This turns out to be part of the air-intake mechanism of the carburettor of a motor car. Or if the term being sought is the name of the piece of armour which covers a knight's shin one can look under the general heading of "Science, Religion and Art" to find "Chivalry" which is illustrated by number 310 and there sure enough is a knight in armour with the shin piece labelled as the *jambart, jambeau* or *greave.*

So the enrichment of context by filling out lexical sets which this book makes possible is very valuable. It does, however, have its own not inconsiderable limitations. Clearly it can only deal with items which are picturable, so that it contains almost nothing but nouns. There *are* a few verbs (relating to athletics, for example—but even here the activities tend to be nominalized) and some colour adjectives, but that is all. There are problems too with interpreting pictures and identifying precisely which part of an illustration is labelled by a particular label number. Many of the illustrations are small in size and densely packed onto the page. The book also shows its origins and its age. The English version uses the definite article before every item, thus "Meadow and Hedgerow Flowers" No 360. lists *the daisy, the marguerite, the cowslip, the knapweed, the yarrow*, etc., presumably exactly paralleling the German version where such usage is appropriate to show gender by the form of the article. The pictures now have a definitely old-fashioned look and the absence of important areas of modern technology is very obvious—there is nothing on computers, video-recording, missiles (apart from a listing under Ethnology—after all, *arrows* are missiles, too!) or solar energy. Nevertheless it is an encyclopaedic and thoroughly useful reference book. It is probably more useful to the teacher or textbook writer than to the elementary learner of English as a foreign language.

Illustrations not only avoid circularity but they clearly enrich context too, as the discussion above of the semantic structuring of vocabulary in the *Duden* shows. It was perhaps partly in pursuit of that kind of structural enrichment that *Roget's Thesaurus* came to be written. As is well known *Roget* is organized under six major conceptual "Classes", Abstract Relations, Space, Matter, Intellect, Volition and Affections. These are further specified in some thirty-nine "sections" which in turn are specified under 990 "heads" (Roget originally had a thousand). Each head is further subdivided into nouns, verbs and adjectives and there are cross references to other related or relevant heads. Access to the enormous vocabulary structured in this way is by way of an alphabetic index which occupies virtually half of the book. Thus as the instructions say:

> If you are sure there is another word for "stamp collector" but cannot bring it to mind, simply look up "stamp collector" in the index at the back of the book which will give a number reference—in this case 492 n. There you will find a range of words relating to the subject, amongst which is the example, "philatelist, stamp collector".

Roget's Thesaurus claims to be a dictionary of synonyms but this claim must be received with some caution. Certainly some heads contain large numbers of synonyms but not all items under one head can always be regarded as synonymous. Take head 492 itself which has the superordinate label "Scholar", and under that "collector" under which we find "bibliophile . . . numismatist, philatelist, stamp collector, . . . lexicographer". It is quite clear that these are species of the genus "collector" and not synonyms for one another, though the appearance of *philatelist* and *stamp collector* side by side does allow their synonymy to appear even though it is not actually marked. This mixture of synonyms and species names is even more obvious under heads like "Animal" which has a sub-head "dog" where breeds of dog are mixed up with various synonyms for dog.

Most people find that it is only through the index that a term being sought can be found. As Robert Ilson has pointed out (Ilson, 1983) to try to work through the conceptual schema to the specific term is very frustrating and turns out to be almost impossible. Part of the difficulty, and perhaps the greatest for learners of English attempting to use *Roget*, is that it doesn't give meanings or usage levels for words; it has always to be used with a dictionary which *does* give these. The semantic structuring is much less clear or accessible than that of the *Duden* for example. *Roget* has a very distinctive nineteenth-century philosophical framework which makes it hard to use in the twentieth century. However it is much richer in its coverage of the English vocabulary including as it does the other major content-word parts of speech, nouns, verbs, adjectives, and adverbs, and all those aspects of feeling and the mind which are not picturable.

It must be recognized that for language learners there are at least two kinds of "context" which have to be considered: real world/cultural context and language-system context. It is real world/cultural context that determines that *fork* may be associated with *spade*, *hoe*, and *earth* or perhaps with *knife*, *spoon*, *plate*, and *food*. It is language-system context that associates "How many _____ are there?" with *forks* and "How much _____ is there?" with *food*. That is to say that part of the language-system context is grammatical. Ordinary learners' dictionaries now deal with this quite well, as for example through the elaborate grammatical coding system used in the *LDOCE*. But the language system also imposes a pattern of lexicalization on the real world. For example, in English certain family relations are specified as *sister* or *uncle*; others are not. In contrast quite other relations may be specified in another language like Swahili where *dada* ("older sister") or *umbu* (only used by brothers of their sisters) and *mjomba* ("maternal uncle") or *amu* ("paternal uncle") are used. Such lexicalization of the realities of biology are arbitrary, though perhaps of course culturally influenced. The arbitrariness goes further than this since it also affects which words "go with" which. A great many types of food may be boiled, but only eggs can be scrambled or shirred, and when the non-English-speaking learner is confronted with the "idiomatic" usages of English, that is when he doesn't know whether he *makes*, *does*, or *has* a *bath*, a *meal*, or his *homework*. The truly idiomatic end of this spectrum is also being increasingly well dealt with in ordinary learners' dictionaries: to take the *LDOCE* again as an example items like "have a bath" are treated as single entities and the apperance of specialized dictionaries like Cowie and Mackin's (1975) *The Oxford Dictionary of Current Idiomatic English*, vol. 1 and LDEI, makes it possible for the learner to cope with such problems reasonably well.

Much more difficult are the collocations which link *galloping*, *cantering* and *trotting* with *horses*, and *prospecting* with *minerals*, *mines*, and *panning*.

One attempt to approach this difficulty has been made by McArthur (1981) with the *Longman Lexicon of Contemporary English*. The basic plan of the *Lexicon* is similar to that of *Roget's Thesaurus*, but instead of the 39 sections of *Roget* there are only 14 "semantic fields" of a "pragmatic everyday nature". Each "field" is identified by a letter code, and subfields by numbers with a system of cross-referencing which isn't quite as complete as perhaps it might be. The coverage of the *Lexicon* focuses on "the central vocabulary of the English Language"—"some 15,000 items". This book too is provided with an index whereby the user may find his way from specific item to general context or semantic field. The conceptual structure seems to be much more contemporary and better defined than in *Roget* so that it is in fact possible to find a specific term within a general field. Thus within the general field A "Life and Living Things" set A50 relates to "Animals/Mammals" and A54 to "Dogs" and a number of particular breeds of dog, for example *Alsatian* can be identified by reference to a labelled illustration. The *Lexicon* is well illustrated, though it uses no colour and this makes treatment of the colour adjectives awkward and indeed "circular" in the technical sense. It will be seen then that the book combines features of the *Duden* and *Roget's Thesaurus*. The *Lexicon* however goes further than this and avoids the problems with meaning which characterize *Roget* since it includes definitions, usage labels, and semantic feature networks—as for example for family relations c12:

Relationship \ Sex	Male	Female
Parent	Father	Mother
Child in relation to parents	Son	Daughter
Child in relation to other children	Brother	Sister

The index has pronunciation indicated by a standard phonemic transcription and the item entries are all grammatically coded using the *LDOCE* system. Altogether the book represents a most welcome and encouraging development among the alternatives to dictionaries.

However there is still something left to be desired in its treatment of collocation, *mines*, *shafts* and *prospecting are* listed under the same semantic set, but *minerals* only appears in the definitions or citations under the head words in these sets, i 113, 114, 115. "The movements and speeds of a horse" are listed under "horse riding" as a form of sport K199 and there are cross-references to the horse as an animal and from there to "horseracing", K200. The cooking of eggs by boiling and scrambling is specified (E 100) but the wide collocational range of *boil* as against *scramble* is barely hinted at, and there are no cross-references from the subsets of Food relating to types of food (that is E36 to 53) to any of the subsets relating to the preparation of food (E 100 to 106). So there is no way of knowing whether a steak is boiled, scrambled, roasted, poached or grilled. The conceptual framework is strong enough to carry a good deal more cross-referencing and this would only enhance the already considerable utility of this book to the foreign learner.

This is definitely a learners' reference book and is likely to help the intermediate-level student to enlarge his English vocabulary rapidly, accurately and efficiently. It looks up to date and does indeed include *computer* (J34) though not *micro-chip*; *missile* (H251) but not *solar panel*. Its major limitation must be the deliberately relatively small coverage of the vast field of English vocabulary. Greater comprehensiveness would certainly make it an invaluable resource but might make it unwieldy. As it stands it is admirable for its specified purpose.

Another interesting piece of work clearly derived from the same kind of thinking as went in to the *Longman Lexicon* is the *Topic Dictionary* of Bennett and Van Veen (1981). This is a much less ambitious work than the *Lexicon*. It covers some 32 topic areas and includes 3300 items including idioms and proverbs. It is probably not strictly a reference work but is more like a vocabulary-development exercise book which can be worked through systematically to build or reinforce the learners' vocabulary. The exercise types included in it are sentence completion, matching item and definition, giving synonyms/antonyms, and the listing of the principal parts and tenses of verbs. The book contains simple labelled illustrations—like the *Duden*, though they are not nearly so elaborate or comprehensive—and the exercises, which have the answer key on the same page as it were, in the form of the illustrations with their labels, provide contexts which demonstrate the collocational potential of items at an elementary level rather well (Cf. Lamy, this volume, p. 32—ed.]. Thus Topic 13 *A Day at the Races* includes an exercise which establishes that "When a horse runs fast it gallops. When it doesn't go so fast it trots" etc. This is a book for beginners. It assumes an initial vocabulary level of only 300 words. At that level the avoidance of circularity and the richness of context which are achieved are very well worth while.

A feature of both the last two books mentioned as alternatives to ordinary dictionaries has been the limited vocabulary range within which they have operated. The question then is how that limited vocabulary was arrived at. Clearly one boundary was set by limiting the range of topics treated, but within a topic area it would seem that some kind of criterion of "usefulness" must have been employed. Perhaps the only truly objective means by which usefulness can be determined, at least in part, is by determining the frequency with which items occur in the language. The classic work on the frequency of vocabulary items in English was carried out in the early part of this century culminating in the publication of *The Interim Report on Vocabulary Selection* in 1936 based on the proceedings of a conference sponsored by the Carnegie Corporation in New York in 1934. The *Interim Report* was the basis of two important works on vocabulary frequency. The first was Thorndike and Lorge's *Teachers' Word Book of 30,000 Words*, the second was Michael West's *General Service List of English Words*. The first is a rather difficult book to learn to use, the second is much more accessible and has proved to be one of the most influential of all the books published since the Second World War relevant to TESOL. It has provided input to a very large number of text-books written in this period, and remains one of the principal tools for all those who attempt to write within a restricted vocabulary or to devise criteria for those who do.

The list of 2000 headwords which it contains was selected by West, precisely as the title suggests, as a list for "general-service" English. The information it contains concerning the frequency of use of items has not so far been improved upon by any generally and widely available reference book—though there are a number of research reports and pieces of work in progress which could lead to the production of such a reference work. For each item the gross frequency of its occurrence in five million running words is indicated. Thus GAME is said to occur 638 times, BALL 512 times, and so on. The value of the book does not end there, for the percentage of occurrences which have a particular meaning is also indicated. Thus GAME with the meaning "competition" as in "a game of football," or "a game of cards" accounts for 38% of the 638 occurrences while the meaning "a particular contest" as in "We won six games to three" accounts for 23% of those occurrences, and the meaning "fun" as in "to make game of" accounts for only 0.5% of the occurrences. It is thus fairly easy to infer which of the several meanings is likely to be the most useful to teach in terms of the frequency with which it may be encountered. The teacher or course/text-book writer can of course judge the usefulness of an item on other grounds and may choose to include or exclude a word or a meaning of a word for any number of reasons other than frequency of occurrence, but the *General Service English List* provides basic information which permits such decisions to be made with awareness and not just on the basis of gut feeling.

The list does of course have its limitations and the user needs to be well aware of these. Most important is perhaps the age of the work and of the material on which it was based. All the sources for the frequency count were written: tape-recordings were essentially unavailable and transcriptions of chunks of spoken data were hard to come by at the time the count was done almost 50 years ago. The materials chosen were even then rather archaic and some items seem almost bizarre. They included concordances of *The Bible*, Shakespeare, Wordsworth, Tennyson, Cowper, Pope and Milton, 10 chapters of *Black Beauty*, 3 chapters of *Little Women*, one issue of *Youth's Companion*, The Constitution of the United States, the Garden and Farm Almanac for 1914, and a variety of school text-books in different subjects. It is probably time the General Service English list was updated. Something like the Longman *Lexicon* with frequency tags would be enormously useful.

The reference works discussed in this article are perhaps a rather idiosyncratic selection of "alternatives to dictionaries" for teachers and learners of English as a foreign language—"dictionaries" here referring to such things as bilingual dictionaries, and monolingual learners' dictionaries of the types discussed in Section 1 of this volume. There are of course many other types of dictionary which could be useful to the foreign learner and which might perhaps be regarded as "alternatives". There is the vast range of specialized dictionaries relating to specific subject fields, dictionaries for the sciences (botany, chemistry, or physics), for geography, economics, law, linguistics and so on; there are dictionaries relating to particular features or uses of language—slang, idiom, rhyme, spelling or pronunciation; and a great wealth of reference works which are encyclopaedic and focus on knowledge rather than words but which inevitably contribute to the growth of vocabulary since words are the principal means by which knowledge is transmitted. One looks out over this rich field and thinks of what the future may hold. Is the day of the printed dictionary passing? Must we look forward to that of the electronic word information-retrieval device? The possibilities are certainly exciting— computer storage of vocabulary with very rich contexts of citation in both spoken and written media, frequency marking of meanings of items, provision of multilingual equivalences or cultural explanations, colour illustrations with movement either through high-quality computer graphics or video-disc recording, collocational network referencing, even item-use practice exercises all written in to one integrated program/data base and available for display on screen and/or through sound channel at the touch of a QWERTY (typewriter-like) key-board. It would seem the technology is almost available—will we ever see it used?

References

Bennett, S. M. & Van Veen, T. G. *The Topic Dictionary*, Nelson, 1981.

Cowie, A. P. & Mackin, R. *The Oxford Dictionary of Current Idiomatic English* (vol. 1), Oxford University Press, 1975.

The English Duden, 2nd revised edn., Harrap, 1959.

Ilson, R. "Review of *Roget's Thesaurus* (6th edn. ed. Susan Lloyd)". *ELTJ* **37.2.** pp 187–189.

Lloyd, S. (ed.) *Roget's Thesaurus*, 6th edn., Longman, 1982.

The Longman Dictionary of English Idioms, Longman 1979 (LDEI).

McArthur, T. *The Longman Lexicon of Contemporary English*, Longman, 1981.

Procter, P. *et al.* (eds.) *The Longman Dictionary of Contemporary English*, Longman, 1978.

Thorndike, E. L. & Lorge, I. *The Teacher's Word Book of 30,000 Words*, Teachers College, Columbia University Press, 1944.

West, M. *The Interim Report on Vocabulary Selection*, P. S. King & Co., 1936.

West, M. *A General Service List of English Words*, Longman, 1953.

IV. FROM THEORY TO PRACTICE

FROM FIRST IDEA TO FINISHED ARTEFACT: THE GENERAL EDITOR AS CHIEF ENGINEER

CHARLES McGREGOR

Publisher

Introduction

Dictionaries are like engineering feats. They must first be conceived and then written: first designed and then constructed. Some generalizations about project management apply as well to the making of dictionaries as to the building of bridges.

Yet very little is said in the literature that I have seen about design as the first in a two-phase process, or about procedures in the second phase (writing), or how general administrative principles may be applied to the making of dictionaries. Most articles contain ideas about elements in design, and ignore the processes by which the artefact is made.

This paper discusses these processes, and offers a way of organizing the making of a dictionary.

1. A Scheme

Work on any large undertaking can be divided into two parts. In the first, you think about what to do and how best to do it; in the second, you do it. The first phase has many names: *planning*, *pre-investment study*, *project preparation* are terms used in management literature and the internal documents of international aid organizations, for example. The second is called fairly generally *implementation*.

2. Phase 1: Planning

Planning is the design phase, for creating both the text specifications and the way the whole text will be written. The whole design will not spring fully-formed into your mind: you, the general editor or project leader, will start with a general outline and fill in details bit by bit. This applies as much to the

123

building of a linguistic analysis as to the making of a schedule or a budget. The following is a step-by-step sequence for this phase:

(1) Plan A—first sketch of work, schedule and budget during phases 1 and 2;
(2) Pre-pilot Study—detailed specifications of the text;
(3) Plan B—revision of Plan A;
(4) Pilot Study—writing about 3% of the text;
(5) Plan C—revision of Plan B.

In phase 2, Plan C is implemented.

A rule-of-thumb for the division of resources between Planning and Implementation is to give 5% to Planning and the rest to Implementation. The bulk of the costs in the first phase fall in stage 4: the Pilot Study. (Omit this at your peril: at this stage, you build your small-scale model and test it in conditions that imitate as closely as possible those for full-scale production.)

Explanations and examples for each of the stages of Planning follow, and Figure 1 illustrates them.

2.1 Plan A

This lists the resources needed, showing their distribution over time and between different components of the whole work. It states only general intentions on textual features.

Here is a way of arriving at that list. Start with a total for the whole, in units of work. (These units should be editor-weeks: a work-package of one compiler's output over one week is more appropriate than a shorter one, e.g. a day's work by one compiler, because general areas need to be blocked out at this stage, rather than every detail described and put in place.) Then divide the

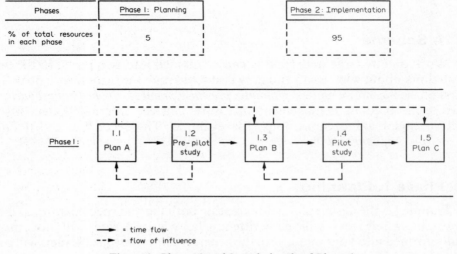

Figure 1. *Phases 1 and 2, with details of Phase 1*

text into a number of equal parts—e.g. into quarters—and sub-divide again. Now divide the total in editor-weeks into the same number of equal parts, and see if the result makes sense, as weekly rates of output and as a total period of work with a sensible number of writers and checkers.

Figure 2 shows how this might be done for a bilingual dictionary, and the next paragraph explains the process in more detail.

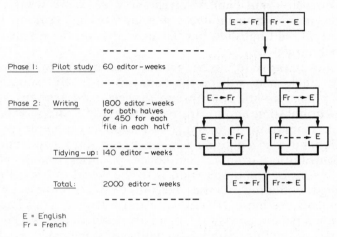

Phase 1:   Pilot study   60 editor-weeks

Phase 2:   Writing   1800 editor-weeks
for both halves
or 450 for each
file in each half

Tidying-up: 140 editor-weeks

Total: 2000 editor-weeks

E = English
Fr = French

Figure 2. *Some details from Plan A*

Suppose, for example, you mean to write a new dictionary comparing French and English, with 50,000 entries plus translations in the French–English part and 50,000 entries with translations in the English–French part, totalling about 18 million characters in all. Past experience suggests a rough total for the work: 2000 editor-weeks. Now you begin to divide the text. First, you split it into two halves: the French–English and the English–French. Then you split each of these into two according to the language: so in the French–English half you distinguish the French entries (which you might call collectively the French source-file) from their English translations (in the aggregate, the English target-file).[1]* We return now to the total of editor-weeks. Deduct 10% (200 editor-weeks), for final tidying-up and for the start-up period (including the Pilot Study): that leaves 1800, which you divide down the middle, giving 900 to each half. Within each half, you allocate the 900 equally so that in the French–English half, you allow 450 editor-weeks to making the French source-file and 450, to the English target-file. Now you look at the weekly rate in a different unit: numbers of completed entries. 450 editor-weeks for preparing 50,000 entries means about 110 entries per editor-week—means, that is, that one editor working for one week should produce around 110 entries. On the English target-file, you are expecting the same rate of weekly output per editor: 110–112 completed translations. These weekly figures certainly look possible, so now you move to consider the calendar periods over which the work will be spread. Assuming 40 working weeks in a calendar year,

* Superscript numbers refer to Notes at end of article.

you find that writing the French source-file will take four editors about 2.8 years. This first piece of rough calculation has produced figures which look at least plausible; now you sit down to much more detailed planning, keeping a careful list of all your heroic assumptions, and you arrive at a schedule showing for each letter of the alphabet when its entries for the French source-file will be written and when its English translations will be done. The same analysis is done for the English–French half.[2] You can now see exactly what work is to be done (by how many) in each week of each working year on the French source-file and on the English target-file, as well as on the English source-file and the French target-file.

At this stage you move to the budget and look first at costs.

The largest single item will be the editorial costs. But support staff are needed, and premises with appropriate services, and perhaps an advisory board, and no doubt some administrative services too. "Support staff" include clerical and electronic data processing (EDP) staff; every employee will expect not only a salary but also a national insurance contribution, paid holidays and a pension contribution from his employer; premises require heating and lighting and means of communication with the world outside. Preparations cost something too: finding premises, recruiting (and training) staff, analysing EDP requirements, testing EDP hardware and software. Travel expenses will be incurred when personnel visit the main areas where the two languages are spoken. As part of the Pilot Study, you will want some page designs done, to see how the finished work will appear and as a check on length. (The page will carry a known number of characters per page; with this knowledge, you can allocate numbers of characters per alphabetic letter—provided you have decided on the number of pages per letter—and can check these totals against actual output as the work proceeds.)

When these compilation costs are totalled, you need to know if they are appropriate. Working that out requires a knowledge of all costs and all revenues: in the private sector of a market economy, expected total revenues must exceed estimated total costs by an appropriate amount in a certain period of time. Total costs include all production costs (the costs of turning the compiled text into pages of characters on a film, of printing these onto the right paper, and of binding the result into books). Other costs are those of finance and administration, of promotion, and of order fulfilment (or warehousing and distribution). Total revenues are a multiple of the number of copies sold and the revenue per copy which the publisher receives. (The number of copies is the sum of those sold in all countries of the world—in the example above, mainly in anglophone and francophone countries. The revenue per copy is the price which the bookshop charges the customer minus the discount that the bookshop receives for stocking the books.) The difficult part in forecasting revenues is guessing accurately the number of copies which will be sold each year.

When the expected total revenues in each of the first five years have been calculated, the production, finance and administration, promoting and order fulfilment costs are deducted, to leave a residue. Over a five-year period, the sum of these annual residues should exceed the total compilation costs by a sufficient amount. If in your budget it does not, then adjustments are needed, by raising the expected revenues, or lowering anticipated costs, or both.

2.2 Pre-pilot Study

In this, you specify what kinds of item to include, how each will be presented, and what data about each will be given. But before you can do this, you must have established your chief objective: to provide a better dictionary for a specified group of readers. This implies that you understand well the important features of this group: the reading materials which they need to understand, and their performance level in writing/reading (since the dictionary will be little consulted for the spoken form, except as written in novels, plays, newspapers). It also implies that you know well the salient textual features of current dictionaries. With this knowledge in mind, you begin to provide details of these superior editorial features, in the form of a Style-Guide for compiling editors.

Since most readers will be familiar with the general structure of dictionary entries, and with their arrangement within the whole dictionary, I shall not plod through these in any detail. Figures 3.1 and 3.2 present the areas for decision diagrammatically, and in a certain order, and the remaining paragraphs in this section explain some elements in these figures.

First, a note on terms. I use *Macrostructure* as J. Rey-Debove (1971) does, to refer to all the headwords (or items to be explained) collectively; the microstructure is represented by all the associated articles (or explanations) [Cf. Lamy, this volume, note 4—ed.]. The choice about macrostructure are primary, with those on microstructure being secondary: first decide a headword is to be included, and only then do decisions arise about what to say

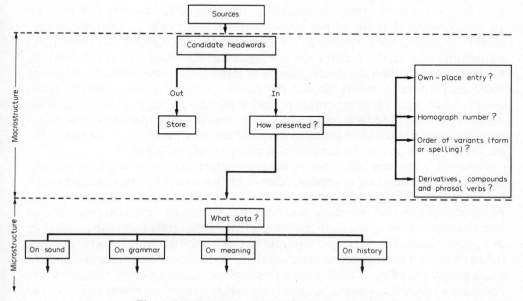

Figure 3.1. *Decisions in Pre-pilot Study—General*

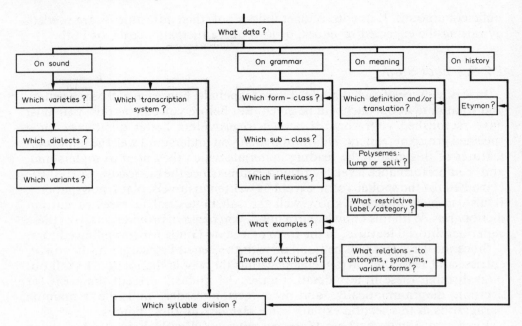

Figure 3.2. *Decisions in Pre-pilot Study—Microstructure*

on it, and how. That first-order decision is not easy to make; but this is not the place to discuss how such decisions may be improved.

Once an item has been chosen for inclusion, other choices on macrostructure may be necessary. Figure 3.1 lists under *How presented* the maximum range: the entry for e.g. *put* requires decisions on three of the four points (not on variants), while that for *turnip* involves none. *Put* exists as verb, noun and adjective: should each appear as separate headwords, or as three sub-entries under only one headword? If each is a separate headword, should the verb be the first (as *put¹*), then the noun (*put²*), and lastly the adjective (*put³*), or should there be a different order? Should the phrasal verbs (e.g. *put aside*) be listed under the verb *put* or as separate entries? With *turnip*, none of these questions arises. But rules need to be made on how to answer each question, so that *put* may be better treated than in competing dictionaries, and so that the treatment of, for example, *get* in the same text is comparable with *put*.

Figure 3.2 lists the full span on microstructure. The article on even *turnip* involves more than might appear. Should both variant pronunciations in RP be included—'tɜːnɪp and 'tɜːnəp? Should it be allocated simply to the noun-class, or should this class be subdivided, so that the uncountable form, as food (*Another helping of turnip, please*), is listed separately from the countable, as a plant? Should there be two separate senses for the countable, as plant in the field and as root on the greengrocer's stall, or should both be subsumed under a more general heading? Dealing with so simple-seeming an entry requires more rules to be made than might be expected; making rules to answer fully each of the listed questions takes several editor-weeks. Perhaps it is not surprising that the final "Editor's Guide" for the German–English Muret Sanders, covering macrostructure and microstructure, ran to 246 pages.

2.3 Plan B

Dusting out Plan A, you wonder: "Can the detailed text I now envisage be written in the time and with the procedures and resources listed there?"

For the macrostructure, the selection and ordering of headwords may (you see now) require outside sources and more work inside. Someone else's citation files may be available, at an acceptable price but an additional cost. Reference to a particular data bank of specialist terms may now be necessary, and the shuffling of individual specialist entries into one alphabetic sequence may now be done more efficiently by EDP than manually.

In the microstructure, the kinds of information chosen may entail a change in required resources. A more deft description of verb complementation may take more/less time to write. Suppose extensive cross-references to words of related meaning are desired: individual meanings may be better described if the members of the same meaning-group are all dealt with by one editor in immediate sequence, rather than each by a different editor at widely separated points in time, following alphabetic order. How can such a change in compiling procedure be organized, and what will be the effects on costs and deadlines?

Items in the schedule may need adjustment for other reasons. The details of the text may suggest a rise or fall in the weekly rate of output per editor—in other words, a higher/lower quantity of editor-weeks for each segment of text. That means changes in the Pilot Study as well as in Phase 2 (Implementation), to schedule and to budget. Perhaps the more detailed design of text has now revealed a fresh EDP contribution: some operations of text integration that were expected to be done manually can now be done automatically, with no change in cost but a gain in elapsed time.

The schedule may need adjustment because of new views on the rate of other editorial functions. For simplicity, I have assumed entries are written in their final form by all compiling editors. But some editors know more than others, and so can handle more complicated entries; and all entries need to be checked by at least one other mind before being captured. Thus the editorial team will have more than one tier in it; in the top tier, the editors will both write the more difficult entries and check those of their peers and juniors. The more original are the forms of the text, the more unpredictable will be both the rates of entry-writing at this stage and the length of training needed for new entrants to the compiling team.

Here as elsewhere, the problem is to keep in mind all these little particulars and their inter-relations, without over-loading your mental channels and slipping into confusion.

When Plan B is done, it is time to begin the Pilot Study.

2.4 Pilot Study

As indicated earlier, the intention here is to test as many elements in the plan as possible, and to arrange that all the important conditions of Phase 2 are reproduced. The design work is tested as a small-scale model, in real-life conditions rather than in the chambers of the mind: do the results show that the features of the new text make it better than existing ones for the intended readers, and that it can be built under the conditions envisaged?

The ideal way to conduct this study is as follows. Assemble the nucleus of the future writing team[3] in the premises to be used, with skeleton support staff but using the actual systems planned (for data entry and data processing, and for reporting). Then arrange for the writing of first 1% of the future text (e.g. the whole of letter J), and then 2% (e.g. the letter N). Have the entries checked, and captured as electronic data, according to plan, and send the print-out to your advisory board, for comment.

Now examine the outcome, as a mini-project in its own right. Are the qualities of the text as expected? What variances appeared between planned (intermediate) deadlines and actual, and between planned costs and actual? What caused these variances? What do they imply for the schedule and budget of Plan B for Phase 2, Implementation?

As you find answers to these question, you are moving into the next stage: preparing Plan C.

2.5 Plan C

Some of the answers may diminish the resemblances between the textual features of the model and those of the full-scale version, or between the conditions under which the model was produced and those for full production. If key text specifications are changed, output rates by editors become more uncertain, together with their associated costs and deadlines. If physical surroundings, or conditions of work, or rates of pay, are altered now, collective attitudes and morale may suffer, affecting textual quality or rates of writing. If the EDP contribution is changed, the distance between its predicted and its actual performance is still unknown.

Even if specifications are little changed, the contingency allowances in Plan B need careful review now. People leave projects unexpectedly (because of illness, outside promotion, psychic crises); institutions undergo unforeseeable changes which affect staffing levels and the use of premises; analytic systems which work with 3% of a population (of lexical units) can fail on the remaining 97%.

Now may be the time to answer another category of "what if?" question. What if during Phase 2 costs over-run or deadlines are missed? The range of remedial action is limited: a higher estimate and/or a later completion date for the whole project may be accepted, which is hardly remedial action, or the project's specifications may be reduced, a thing easily said but hard to do. Another option—less rational but offering at times a deeper release from psychic tension—is to sacrifice a scape-goat, identified in advance by the system of distributed responsibilities among members of the project team: to replace the general editor by another project leader, for example.

When Plan C finally satisfies you, because text quality is right, schedules, costs and operating procedures are appropriate, and the description of all is sufficiently detailed for proper control during Implementation: then the design phase is finished. Now for the full-scale writing.

3. Phase 2: Implementation

It is only now that you find out how good your work in the design phase was. Projects that fail do so more often from poor design than from lapses of control during the writing. (Still, the pains of struggling to implement a faulty design etch the principles of good design more deeply into the sufferer's mind.) Designs may fail because the quality of the text is low—the work merely imitative in conception, though executed on time and within budget; or the design may embody a new linguistic vision most finely, but grossly underestimate the resources needed, and so the project is never finished, its leader another Ozymandias.

But projects can fail from poor control also. This may be the result of a poorly-designed reporting system, itself a reproach to the designer, or from failure to work an adequate system properly. A good reporting system provides the data needed for control at the right intervals and with little extra work for the editors. If for example you want to know how much work each contributor has done each working day, you might put a space for the contributor's initials and the date of the work on the form used for each entry, and arrange for these to be entered with the lexical unit and the article concerned; then with a suitable program you can retrieve a weekly list of work done per contributor at low cost. You might have this printed out with two other columns, showing the planned output for the period and any variance between actual and planned (and incidentally link the reporting of editorial costs to the same record, since this will be just a multiple of the days worked and the daily payment). These weekly records might be summed each month, with a signficant additional column: this would show the current estimate of costs and deadlines for the entire project, compared with those planned.[4] (Make a rule that this estimate contains two components: (1) the actual costs to date and (2) an estimate of all future ones, which is equal to or greater than the estimate in the plan.)

The problem in control is to achieve all three points in the magic triangle of quality,[5] time and cost. If you get behind on deadlines, you can catch up only by taking on more people, so staying on plan for time and (maybe) quality but overshooting costs; or you may just force people to work faster, and make the deadlines and the budgeted costs but sacrifice quality. At your monthly meetings you need to review any variances in each of the three together as well as separately.

The easiest projects to control are those with familiar, well-tested designs and team members who have worked together before on comparable projects. Such projects usually continue a tradition, rather than starting a new one. Yet for some of us, there is more excitement in the novel, the project with more originality in design: the glory of achieving it is greater.

Such achievements require however success in realms beyond those considered in this paper. The text must look attractive; the price must be perceived as fair; the book must be effectively promoted and efficiently distributed. Only then will its publication advance good lexicography, with its sponsor well rewarded, its writers applauded and its readers that much wiser in the language it describes.

Notes

1. Not all publishers divide the work into source and target-files. Langenscheidt, for example, regards the complete entry as the working unit for the editor.
2. Two facts must now be confronted:
    (a) Some entries are more difficult to write than others, so that for example the entry for the verb *put* will take longer than for *turnip*;
    (b) These difficult entries are distributed unequally among the letters of the alphabet.
    As a result, the work for each alphabet (e.g. French–English or English–French) must be divided into 26 individual parts, not 26 equal units.
3. Recruiting people with the right aptitudes, prior knowledge and qualities of mind is not easy. You have first to define these mental features, and then find ways of detecting them in applicants.
4. Self-control by each contributor is the ideal, with the EDP system providing facilities for him or her which manual methods never could. Each contributor would draft his entry, and then consult the editorial material already on file, to ensure the consistency of the draft with this. After that, he would put in his entries as final text, subject to checking by a senior editor. In the same period, he or she would call up a report showing, for example, how his own schedule of delivered entries so far compared with that planned. Used in this way, the EDP system is the contributor's assistant, rather than his overseer.
5. The quality must be appropriate to the readership concerned. A common difficulty is that writers provide too much detail, e.g. too many derivatives, too many neologisms, too many examples, and so cover too few entries in the time available. Such over-writing may emerge first in the pilot study, but may not be finally corrected then.

Reference

Rey-Debove, J., *Etude linguistique et semiotique des dictionnaires français contemporains*. The Hague, Mouton, 1971, pp 20–21.

Acknowledgements

I am grateful to the following for comments on the draft of this paper:

Robert Ilson (editor of this volume),
Richard Charkin (Oxford University Press),
Pierre Cousin (Lexus and Collins),
Alain Duval (consultant to Robert),
Federico Enriques (Zanichelli),
Wolfgang Kaul (Ernst Klett),
Ole Norling-Christensen (Gyldendal),
Della Summers (Longman),
Richard Thomas (Collins),
Walter Voigt (Langenscheidt),
Janet Whitcut (contributor).

NOTES ON CONTRIBUTORS

Beryl T. Atkins, a lexicographer with Collins Publishers, is a General Editor of the Collins-Robert series of English/French dictionaries and General Editor of the Cobuild Project of computerised lexicographical research into current English and the needs of the learner. She is co-author with Tom McArthur, of *Dictionary of English Phrasal Verbs*, and is currently concerned with research into dictionary use by learners, on behalf of EURALEX (the European Association for Lexicography).

Marton Benson is Professor of Slavic Languages and a member of the Graduate Group in Linguistics, University of Pennsylvania. He teaches a course on "Lexicography: the Description of Modern English" and is author of the *Dictionary of Russian Names* (1964, 1967), the *SerboCroatian-English Dictionary* (1971, 1979), the *English-SerboCroatian Dictionary* (1979) and articles in various journals. He is also co-author of the *Lexicographic Description of English* and *Combinatory Dictionary of English* (Benjamins, forthcoming).

Dwight Bolinger is Professor Emeritus of Romance Languages and Literatures, Harvard University and Visiting Professor Emeritus of Linguistics, Stanford University. He is now in his eleventh year of active retirement. His current interest is prosody, especially intonation, with one volume (*Intonation and Its Parts: Melody in Spoken English*) soon to be published by Stanford Press, and a second in preparation.

C. P. Hill is Senior Lecturer, ESOL Department, London University Institute of Education. He has also been Director of the London University Summer School of English for seven years. He is a member of the Royal Society of Arts Advisory Committee on TESOL teachers' certificates, lecturer/tutor on many British Council summer courses and co-author of *Teaching English as a Foreign Language* (RKP) and *Language in Tanzania*.

Robert Ilson, Editor of this volume, is an Honorary Research Fellow of University College London and an Associate Director of the Survey of English Usage. He has been the Managing Editor of LDOCE (UK), a General Editor of *The Second Barnhart Dictionary of New English* (USA), and the Consultant Editor of *Reader's Digest Great Illustrated Dictionary* (UK).

Howard Jackson studied German at King's College London and the University of Freiburg, then Linguistics at the University of Reading, with a PhD thesis on the subclassification of verbs in English and German. He now teaches Linguistics at the City of Birmingham Polytechnic. He is author of the textbooks *Analyzing English, an introduction to descriptive linguistics* (Pergamon, 1982) and *Discovering Grammar* (Pergamon, forthcoming). His linguistic interests include Contrastive Analysis and Valency Grammar.

Betty Kirkpatrick, editorial director of W. & R. Chambers, was head of the dictionaries team which has compiled such works as *Chambers Universal Learners' Dictionary* and revised the long-established *Chambers 20th Century Dictionary*. She has also worked in the field of children's dictionaries and in that of biographical and technical dictionaries. A lover of language as well as of lexicography, she is the chief adjudicator at the National Scrabble Championship and writes a regular column on words for the *Glasgow Herald*.

Marie-Noëlle Lamy is a bilingual lexicographer; she was one of the editors of the *Collins-Robert French-English Dictionary*. She lectured at Salford University for nine years, and has published and taught about lexicography. She is currently involved in a new bilingual project for Cassell's and is a Visiting Fellow of Salford University, where she teaches the Lexicography element on the post-graduate language course.

Charles McGregor has worked in British educational publishing for the last 20 years, specializing as a manager in language-teaching materials and in books for primary and secondary schools in Africa. He is a Sloan Fellow of the London Business School, and an Oxford graduate in Animal Physiology. His past appointments include project manager for LDOCE, in Longman.

Richard Rossner is Director of Studies at the Bell School, Cambridge and editor of *ELT Journal* (published by the OUP in association with the British Council). He is co-author of a number of EFL textbooks, notably *Contemporary English* (Macmillan). He has been interested in the problems of vocabulary learning and teaching for several years, and has been working (on and off) on the problems of describing words and organizing activities and materials to facilitate the learning of them.

John Sinclair has since 1965 been Professor of Modern English Language, University of Birmingham, where he is also Director of the Cobuild Project of computerised lexicographical research into current English and the needs of the learner. He has had previous education and experience in Edinburgh, and has current research interests in discourse analysis and text linguistics. He is also involved in post-experience courses for teachers of English.

Professor Gabriele Stein holds the chair of English Linguistics at the University of Hamburg, West Germany.

Adrian Underhill is in-service teacher trainer and teacher of EFL at International House, Hastings. His work is directed towards exploring the possibilities of humanistic education, and helping learners and teachers to evolve their own most effective ways of working. He is engaged in studying the

active use of the MLD in the classroom, and its potential to help learners take more responsibility for their learning. He is author of *Use Your Dictionary*, OUP.

John Christopher Wells is Reader in Phonetics at University College London, and author of *Accents of English* (3 vols., CUP 1982) and other works. He is also secretary of the International Phonetic Association and Editor of its Journal.

Janet Whitcut taught EFL for some years, examining and setting examinations, particularly in English Usage, for the Cambridge Board and ARELS. She worked on the Survey of English Usage team under Professor Sir Randolph Quirk, and was an editor of LDOCE, and the *Longman Active Study Dictionary* and the Managing Editor of the *Longman New Generation Dictionary*. She has published a workbook and tape to accompany LDOCE, and is now revising Ernest Gowers' Complete Plain Words for HM Stationery Office.